SPANISH GRAMMAR

for Key Stages 3 and 4

Melanie Navarro-Marín

Mary Glasgow Publications

An imprint of S......... (Publishers) Ltd

First published in 1996 by:
Mary Glasgow Publications, an imprint of Stanley Thornes (Publishers) Ltd

Reprinted in 2001 by:
Nelson Thornes Ltd
Delta Place
27 Bath Road
CHELTENHAM
GL53 7TH
United Kingdom

01   02   03   04   05   /   10   9   8   7

A catalogue record for this book is available from the British Library

ISBN 0 7487 2226 2

Illustrations by Shaun Williams
Page make-up by TechSet

Printed and bound in Great Britain by The Bath Press

Contents

Introduction

Understanding how a language works is a vital part of learning that language. Once you can understand the grammar system, you will be able to use the language more fully and with more confidence.

If you are in your first few years of learning Spanish and you are looking for some help in getting to grips with its grammar, then this is the book for you.

The Key to Spanish Grammar offers you a step-by-step approach to the main grammar points you will need to know at a basic to intermediate level of Spanish. Each section contains activities to enable you to apply the grammar you are learning. Answers are included at the back.

Key

 **¡Atención!**   Particularly important points to take note of

¿Entiendes?   Revision activities on the grammar points

Resumen   A summary of the grammar points covered

Using this book

Here are a few tips for using *The Key to Spanish Grammar*:

- Don't try to read it from cover to cover!

- Get an exercise book or a file and label it 'My Key to Spanish Grammar'. When you learn a new grammar point, write it down. You may be able to write it in a way which is particularly easy for you to understand and remember.

- If there is a grammar point you are unsure about, or you want to learn, look it up in the contents page, turn to the relevant page in the book and work your way through the step-by-step explanations.

- As you come across new grammar points in your Spanish lessons, look them up in this book for further help.

- Do the *¿Entiendes?* exercises and check your answers in the back to see if you really have understood the explanations.

- Make learning cards for grammar points you find hard to remember. Write the explanations or the patterns on pieces of card. Keep these cards in different places. Whenever you have a spare moment, pick up the cards and test yourself on the grammar.

- Keep on revising the grammar you have learned. Note down the key points on a piece of paper and then check in this book to see if you have remembered everything correctly.

- Do try and learn some of the grammar patterns. Maybe you can think up rhymes or sentences to help you do this.

- You can learn grammar with a friend. One of you can look at this book while the other one explains the grammar point. Alternatively, the person with the book can ask the other person quiz questions on the grammar.

- Have this book in front of you when you do your written homework. You can refer to it as you go – and afterwards – to check what you are writing.

- Don't worry if you can't remember all the grammar points. You can always refer back to this book for help or ask your teacher in your next Spanish lesson.

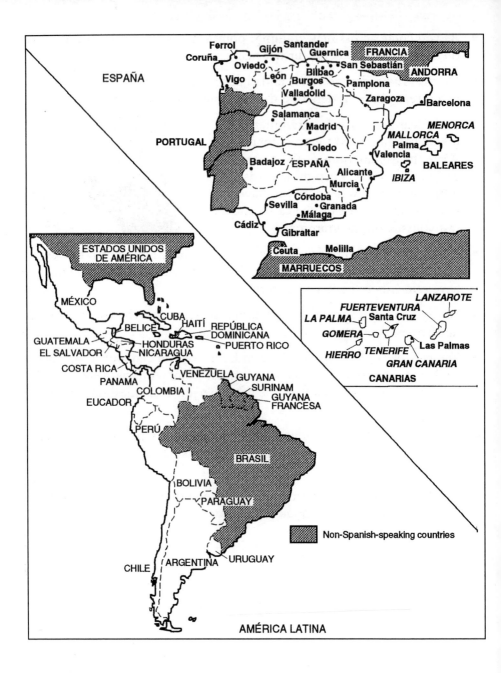

1 Using *un*, *uno* and *una*

1 In Spanish there are three words for 'a', 'an' or 'one': **un**, **una**, and **uno**.

Un and **uno** are masculine.
Una is feminine.

2 In Spanish nouns are considered to be either masculine or feminine. We do not make this distinction in English. If a Spanish noun is masculine it uses **un** to mean 'a', 'an' or 'one'; if it is feminine it uses **una**. When you learn a new word you should always learn whether it is masculine, and uses **un**, or feminine and uses **una**:

un perro	*a dog*
una hermana	*a sister*

3 **Un** and **uno** are both masculine. You use **un** when it is followed by a noun that is masculine singular (see also note 4):

un gato	*a cat*
un vaso	*a glass*
un huevo	*an egg*
un hermano	*one brother*

4 **Uno** is used to mean 'one' referring to a masculine singular noun when no noun follows it:

¿Cuántos hermanos tienes?	*How many brothers have you got?*
Uno.	*One.*
¿Hay un banco por aquí?	*Is there a bank around here?*
Sí, hay uno.	*Yes, there's one.*

5 **Una** is used with a feminine singular noun:

una mesa	*a table*
una lámpara	*a lamp*
una manzana	*an apple*
una camisa	*one shirt*

6 **Unos** and **unas** both mean 'some' and are the plural of **un/uno** and **una**.

¿Entiendes?

A Write out the following sentences filling in the gaps with either **un**, **uno**, **una**, **unos** or **unas**.

1 ¿Hay ..... farmacia cerca? Sí. Hay ..... enfrente.
2 Tengo ..... caramelos.
3 ¿Dónde hay ..... bar por aquí?
4 Quiero comprar ..... monedero y ..... muñeca.
5 ¿Tienes hermanos? Sí, ...
6 Tienen ..... televisiones grandes.

Resumen

Un, **uno** and **una** mean 'a' (or 'an') or 'one'.
Unos and **unas** mean 'some'.

	singular	plural
masculine	un/uno	unos
feminine	una	unas

2 Using *el, la, los* and *las*

1 In Spanish the word for 'the' can be expressed in four different ways:

el gato *the cat*   los gatos *the cats*
la hamburguesa *the hamburger*   las hamburguesas *the hamburgers*

2 *El* and *la* both mean 'the' when you refer to one object (singular):

el suelo   *the floor*
la puerta   *the door*

- Every noun (i.e. person or object) in Spanish is either masculine or feminine (see Point 3). Masculine nouns take *el*, feminine nouns take *la*.

- When you look up words in a dictionary, you will see that after each noun there is *nm* or *nf*:
  nm = a noun that is masculine (and therefore takes *el*)
  nf = a noun that is feminine (and therefore takes *la*).

3 *Los* and *las* both mean 'the' when you refer to more than one object or person:

Los is masculine; *las* is feminine.
El (masculine singular) changes to *los* (masculine plural).
La (feminine singular) changes to *las* (feminine plural).

⚠ **¡Atención!**

*When some nouns change into the plural, their meaning can be changed slightly. This happens when you talk about some members of the family, e.g.: **el padre** (the father); **los padres** (the parents).*

¿Entiendes?

A Look at these nouns. Change each one into the plural. (In these examples add an **s** to all nouns in the plural. See Point 3.)

Example

el chico   *los chicos*
la chica   *las chicas*

Now do the same for these words. Check your answers.

1 la escalera   5 el libro
2 el zapato   6 la cortina
3 la taza   7 el vaso
4 el teléfono   8 la botella

B **Can you work out what the following mean? Check your answers.**

1 los abuelos
2 los tíos
3 los hermanos
4 los primos

C **If you saw these Spanish words in a dictionary, would they be masculine or feminine? What does each one mean in English? Look at the example:**

perro (*nm*) ⟶ el perro = the dog

Now complete the other words following the example. Check your answers.

1 lápiz (*nm*)   5 banco (*nm*)
2 ratón (*nm*)   6 reloj (*nm*)
3 horno (*nm*)   7 televisión (*nf*)
4 regla (*nf*)   8 flor (*nf*)

Resumen

1 **El**, **la**, **los** and **las** all mean 'the'.

2 Remember:

	singular (one person or thing)	plural (more than one person or thing)
masculine	el	los
feminine	la	las

3 Nouns and adjectives

Nouns

1 A noun is an object, person or thing, e.g.: **un libro** (a book), **una mesa** (a table), **una chica** (a girl).

2 All nouns are either masculine or feminine. As a general rule, if a noun ends in an **o** it is masculine. If it ends in an **a** it is feminine:

un teléfono (masculine)   *a telephone*
una silla (feminine)   *a chair*

However, there are some exceptions to the rule:

- un día   *a day*
  un problema   *a problem*
  un sofá   *a sofa*
  They end in **a** but are masculine.

- una radio   *a radio*
  This ends in **o** but is feminine.

3 How to make a noun plural

- If it ends in a vowel, you add an **s**:

un chico   *a boy* ⟶ unos chicos   *(some) boys*
un disco   *a record* ⟶ unos discos   *(some) records*
una lámpara   *a lamp* ⟶ unas lámparas   *(some) lamps*
una mesa   *a table* ⟶ unas mesas   *(some) tables*

- If it ends in a consonant, then you add **es**:

el tren   *the train* ⟶ los trenes   *the trains*
la canción   *the song* ⟶ las canciones   *the songs*

- There is a group of nouns ending in **z** that form the plural in a different way:

un pez   *a fish* ⟶ unos peces   *(some) fishes*
una vez   *one time* ⟶ unas veces   *(some) times*

As you can see, the **z** changes to **ces** in the plural.

4 Some feminine nouns beginning with an **a** or **ha** which is stressed use the masculine form of the article in the singular:

el agua	*water* (instead of 'la' agua)
el ama de casa	*housewife*
el alma	*soul*

Adjectives

1 An adjective is a word used to describe a noun in some way. It usually goes after the noun in Spanish:

un chico **guapo**	*a handsome boy*
una niña **bonita**	*a pretty girl*
unos perros **traviesos**	*naughty dogs*
unas mujeres **gordas**	*fat women*

2 An adjective needs to agree with the noun it is describing (whether it is masculine or feminine, singular or plural).

- If an adjective ends in an **o** in the masculine singular, it will have four forms. There are no exceptions to this pattern, e.g. **simpático** (kind):

masculine singular	feminine singular	masculine plural	feminine plural
simpático	simpática	simpáticos	simpáticas

- If an adjective ends in a consonant, then the masculine and feminine singular forms do not change. In the plural you add **es**:

un calcetín azul	*a blue sock*
una chaqueta azul	*a blue jacket*
unos calcetines azules	*blue socks*
unas chaquetas azules	*blue jackets*

3 **Apocopation** is the technical word used for a very simple process. Some adjectives can be used before the noun. When they are placed there, the masculine singular form is shortened. This is done so that the meaning of the adjective is stressed, e.g. **un buen amigo** (a good friend).

The only adjectives that change in this way are:

bueno	⟶	buen (good)
malo	⟶	mal (bad)
primero	⟶	primer (first)
tercero	⟶	tercer (third)
uno (see Point 1)	⟶	un (a, an, one)
alguno	⟶	algún (some)
ninguno	⟶	ningún (not any, not a,...)

Note that an accent is placed on both **algún** and **ningún**.

● **Grande** (big, great) is shortened to **gran** when used before any singular noun – masculine or feminine. It is normally used before a noun when it refers to greatness rather than to size:

un hombre **grande**	*a big man*
un **gran** hombre	*a great man*

¿Entiendes?

A Make the following nouns plural. Don't forget to change the **el** or **la** to **los** or **las**.

1 el perro
2 la capital
3 la nariz
4 el reloj
5 el jefe
6 la voz
7 la abuela
8 el mar
9 el pastel
10 la maleta

B Put these sentences into Spanish. Use the adjectives in the box to help you. You will need to change the form of the adjective in some cases!

1 a tall girl
2 red shoes
3 a fat dog

4 slim girls
5 a wide street
6 short hair
7 interesting classes
8 green eyes
9 a pink hat
10 handsome boys

gordo	**rojo**	**delgado**	**verde**
	ancho	**rosa**	**alta**
guapo	**corto**	**interesante**	

c Work out the meaning of the following:

1 un buen hombre
2 en el primer piso
3 el tercer chico
4 un gran hombre
5 ¿Tienes algún dinero?
6 No tengo ningún amigo.

Resumen

A Nouns

1 All nouns are either masculine or feminine.

2 If a noun ends in a vowel, add **s** to make it plural.

3 If a noun ends in a consonant, add **es** to make it plural.

B Adjectives

1 All adjectives need to agree with the noun they are describing.

2 If an adjective ends in **o** in the masculine form, it will follow this pattern:

masc. sing. **-o**   masc.plural **-os**
fem.sing. **-a**   fem.plural **-as**

3 If an adjective ends in a consonant, the masculine and feminine forms do not change but **es** is added to make the adjective plural.

4 Adverbs

1 Adverbs are words that give extra information about the action of a verb:

Él condujo **rápidamente**.   *He drove quickly.*

They can also be used to describe an adjective.

2 In English many adverbs end in 'ly'. In Spanish they follow a similar pattern and end in **mente**:

rápidamente   *quickly*
lentamente   *slowly*

They are easy to form:
- Take an adjective – **seguro** (sure)
- Change it to the feminine singular form (**o** ⟶ **a**) – **segura**
- Add on mente – **seguramente** (surely)

Note that if the adjective used does not have a feminine form, just simply add **mente** onto the singular form:

regular   ⟶ regularmente (regularly)
reciente   ⟶ recientemente (recently)
fácil   ⟶ fácilmente (easily)

¿Entiendes?

A Change the following adjectives into adverbs. Don't forget to check your answers.

1 fácil
2 cierto
3 lento
4 estupendo
5 posible
6 atento
7 probable
8 cuidadoso

B   Now choose an adverb from the box that would suitably describe each sentence.

Example
Ayer llegaste pronto. ¿Cómo condujo tu madre? *Rápidamente.*

1 ¿Cuándo visitaste España? .....
2 Voy todos los días a la piscina. .....
3 Para hacer los deberes tengo que prestar mucha atención. .....
4 A lo mejor saco buenas notas en el examen de español. .....
5 Es seguro que celebraremos mi cumpleaños en la discoteca. .....
6 Mi hermano no puede correr muy rápido. .....

lentamente	**regularmente**	**probablemente**
atentamente	**recientemente**	**ciertamente**

 **¡Atención!**

Note that when you have two adverbs together both ending in **mente***, the* **mente** *is often missed off the first one:*

Mi abuela anda **lenta** *y* **cuidadosamente***. (My grandmother walks slowly and carefully).*

Note that there are some adverbs that do not follow the **-mente** *pattern. These need to be learnt separately.*

c   Match up the list on the left with the list on the right to give you the irregular adverbs. Check your answers.

1	mucho	**a**	a little
2	poco	**b**	very much/a great deal
3	bien	**c**	rarely
4	mal	**d**	badly
5	rara vez	**e**	sometimes
6	muchas veces/a menudo	**f**	a lot
7	algunas veces/a veces	**g**	from time to time
8	nunca	**h**	often
9	muchísimo	**i**	never
10	de vez en cuando	**j**	well
11	cerca	**k**	far
12	allí	**l**	opposite

13 aquí		**m**	nearby
14 lejos		**n**	here
15 enfrente		**o**	there

3 Some adverbs give more precise details or meaning to adjectives or other adverbs:

muy	*very*
bastante	*fairly, quite*
demasiado	*too*

El libro es **muy** interesante.	*The book is very interesting.*
Mi hermano es **bastante** alto.	*My brother is quite tall.*
Mi profesora vive **demasiado** cerca.	*My teacher lives too near.*

Resumen

1 Adverbs are words that describe how the action of a verb is carried out.

2 They are easy to form:
- Take an adjective.
- Change it to the feminine singular form.
- Then add **mente**.

3 Some adverbs are irregular, and need to be learnt separately.

5 Introduction to verbs

1 You will read the word 'verb' lots of times and you therefore need to know what it means. Perhaps you do already. A verb is an action word or a 'doing' word. It explains what exactly is happening, e.g. 'go', 'run', 'sleep'.

2 Verbs are sometimes referred to as being 'in the infinitive'. This simply tells us the name of the verb. It is the part of the verb you find when you look it up in a dictionary. In English, all verbs in the infinitive will have 'to' in front of them, e.g. 'to speak', 'to eat', 'to live'. In Spanish, the infinitive of a verb ends in one of three ways:

-ar, e.g. habl**ar**
-er, e.g. com**er**
-ir, e.g. viv**ir**

3 When studying languages you will often hear the word 'tense'. A 'tense' tells you when something is happening:

Present tense .... Now, this minute.
Past tense .... In the past, yesterday, last week, etc.
Future tense ..... In the future, next week, tomorrow, etc.

4 Verbs can be regular or irregular

- A regular verb is a verb that follows a set pattern and 'behaves' itself.
- An irregular verb is a verb that does not follow a set pattern, is different in some way, and therefore 'misbehaves'!
- Some verbs can be regular in one tense but not in another. They can be irregular in all tenses, or regular in all tenses.
- The more commonly-used verbs tend to be mostly irregular, but they are also quite easy to learn.

5 The word 'conjugate' is simply a technical way of talking about the different forms of the verbs that correspond to different people. Verbs in English can seem to be easier than verbs in other languages. Not necessarily so! In Spanish, things are made easier by being able to follow certain set patterns that usually do not change.

6 In English we talk about 'I', 'you', 'he', 'she', etc. These are called **personal pronouns**. Look at the Spanish equivalents:

Singular			Plural		
I	yo		*we*	nosotros (masc.)/nosotras (fem.)	
you	tú		*you*	vosotros (masc.)/vosotras (fem.)	
he	él		*they*	ellos (masc.)/ellas (fem.)	
she	ella				
you	usted	(polite)	*you*	ustedes	(polite)

Usted (Vd.) is the polite form of the verb when you are talking to one person, usually an adult or somebody you do not know very well. You use **ustedes (Vds.)** when you talk to more than one person in the polite form. Note that they take the same part of the verb as 'he'/'she' (**usted**) and 'they' (**ustedes**).

Look at the verb 'to speak' (**hablar**) set out in the present tense in both English and Spanish. How many things do you notice?

yo habl**o**	*I speak*
tú habl**as**	*you speak*
él/ella/(Vd.) habl**a**	*he/she/it speaks*
	(you speak)
nosotros/as habl**amos**	*we speak*
vosotros/as habl**áis**	*you speak*
ellos/ellas/(Vds.) habl**an**	*they speak*
	(you speak)

You should have noticed the following things:

- In English, the form of the verb only changes when you talk about 'he', 'she' or 'it'.
- In Spanish, every person you speak about has a certain ending.
- Because of the endings mentioned in note 2, the equivalent of 'I', 'you', 'she', etc. are often not used in Spanish. Spaniards know who you are talking about by the ending on the verb.

7 To sum up

- In Spanish you can say **hablo** and, because of the **o** ending, Spanish people know you are talking about yourself.
- Very often the personal pronouns (**yo, tú, él**, etc.) are only used for stressing a certain point or for comparing, e.g.:

13

Yo como poco, pero **tú** comes mucho.   *I eat little, but you eat a lot.*

- Verbs often cause people a lot of problems. The best way to deal with them is to learn the patterns off by heart.
- Verbs in Spanish are easy! They can be learnt as rhymes and in certain patterns.
- Look at some verbs in the present tense in Point 6.

Resumen

1 Verbs describe actions.

2 The infinitive is the verb's 'name', the part you find in the dictionary.

3 Tenses tell you when things happen.

4 Regular verbs follow set patterns.

5 Irregular verbs do not follow set patterns.

6 Personal pronouns tell you who is doing the action. These are often left out in Spanish, so you have to look at the verb ending.

6 The present tense (regular and irregular verbs)

1 The present tense is used in two cases:

A When you want to talk about something that is happening now:
Mamá prepara la comida.   *Mum prepares/is preparing dinner.*

B When you want to talk about something that happens on a regular basis:
Los viernes por la tarde juego al fútbol.
I play football on Friday evenings.

2 The present tense of regular verbs is easy to form. You take the verb in the infinitive (ending **ar**, **er** or **ir**), take off the **ar**, **er** or **ir** ending and add on the endings according to whom you want to talk about.

Look at the endings for **-ar**, **-er** and **-ir** verbs:

Hab**lar**	Com**er**	Viv**ir**
habl**o**	com**o**	viv**o**
habl**as**	com**es**	viv**es**
habl**a**	com**e**	viv**e**
habl**amos**	com**emos**	viv**imos**
habl**áis**	com**éis**	viv**ís**
habl**an**	com**en**	viv**en**

As you can see, the 'I' form of regular verbs always ends in an **o**. All the other **-ar** verb endings have an **a** in them, the **-er** verb endings have an **e** in them, and the **-ir** verbs have some **e** and some **i** endings.

The endings are easy to learn, especially if you learn them as a pattern or rhyme:

-ar verbs	-er verbs	-ir verbs
o	o	o
as	es	es
a	e	e
amos	emos	imos
áis	éis	ís
an	en	en

Look at some examples of the present tense:

Juan habla francés.   *John speaks French.*
Normalmente nosotros comemos a las dos.
                                       Usually we eat at two o'clock.
Mis abuelos viven en Escocia.   *My grandparents live in Scotland.*

3 Unfortunately, some of the most commonly-used verbs are irregular
and very often do not follow any set patterns. These verbs have to be
learnt separately.
Some common verbs are slightly irregular in one part of the present
tense (see Point 9: stem-changing verbs).

A ***Dar*** and ***estar***
The **yo** forms end in **y**:
dar   doy
estar   estoy

B ***Caer, traer, hacer, poner, salir***
The **yo** form gains a **g**:
caer   caigo
traer   traigo
hacer   hago
poner   pongo
salir   salgo

C ***Decir, tener, venir***
These verbs gain a **g** in the **yo** form of the verb, but they are also
stem-changing (see Point 9).
decir   digo
tener   tengo
venir   vengo

D ***Ir, ser***
Some other verbs, like these, are totally irregular (see the Verb Tables
on pages 124-30 for all parts and tenses).

¿Entiendes?

A Write out the message on the postcard, choosing from the verbs in the box
opposite to fill in the gaps. Remember to give them the correct endings!

beber	adorar	llegar	tomar	estudiar
pasar	llevar	escuchar	leer	

Yo ..... las vacaciones de verano. En julio nosotros ..... a la playa temprano y ..... el sol. En la playa, yo ..... Coca-Cola y ..... un libro de aventuras. Mi hermano ..... música. Mis padres ..... una pelota y juegos y todos ..... horas jugando. Mi hermano y yo no ..... .

¡Vivan las vacaciones!

Resumen

1 The present tense describes an action that happens now or on a regular basis:

Mi madre lava los platos.   *My mother washes up/is washing up.*
Los viernes, mi padre prepara la cena.
                            On Fridays, my father prepares dinner.

2 When you look up a verb in the dictionary, the form of the verb that is given will be in the infinitive (ending in **ar**, **er** or **ir**).

3 All regular verbs follow a set pattern. The **ar**, **er**, **ir** are taken off and replaced by:

-ar	-er	-ir
o	o	o
as	es	es
a	e	e
amos	emos	imos
áis	éis	ís
an	en	en

7 Reflexive verbs

1 A reflexive verb is easy to identify. It describes something that you do to or for yourself:

La chica se despierta. *The girl wakes up/wakes herself up.*

2 A lot of reflexive verbs are easy to remember because they explain things that you do every day:

despertarse*	*to wake up*
levantarse	*to get up*
lavarse el pelo	*to wash one's hair*
lavarse	*to wash (oneself)*
bañarse	*to have a bath*
ducharse	*to have a shower*
afeitarse	*to have a shave*
peinarse	*to comb one's hair*
vestirse*	*to get dressed*
ponerse	*to put on*
divertirse*	*to enjoy oneself*
cambiarse	*to get changed*
quitarse la ropa	*to undress*
acostarse*	*to go to bed*
dormirse*	*to fall asleep*

(*) Stem-changing verbs. See Point 9.

All the above verbs are in the infinitive and you should notice that all of them have **se** on the end of the **-ar, -er, -ir** verb. This is the part that shows us that the verb is reflexive and is called a 'reflexive pronoun'. The above construction is used only when the verb is used in the infinitive (see note 4).

3 When you want to talk about 'I', 'he', 'she', etc, the reflexive pronoun **se** is taken off the infinitive and follows a pattern that changes according to whom you are talking about. Look at the examples:

lavarse *to wash oneself (to have a wash)*			
yo	**me** lavo	nosotros/as	**nos** lavamos
tú	**te** lavas	vosostros/as	**os** laváis
él/ella/Vd.	**se** lava	ellos/ellas/Vds.	**se** lavan

ponerse *to put on*			
yo	**me** pongo	nosotros/as	**nos** ponemos
tú	**te** pones	vosostros/as	**os** ponéis
él/ella/Vd.	**se** pone	ellos/ellas/Vds.	**se** ponen

vestirse *to dress*			
yo	**me** visto	nosotros/as	**nos** vestimos
tú	**te** vistes	vosostros/as	**os** vestís
él/ella/Vd.	**se** viste	ellos/ellas/Vds.	**se** visten

Note that when you take off the **se** from *lavarse* you are left with an -*ar* verb which follows the nomal pattern of -*ar* verbs when you talk about different people. **Ponerse** is an -*er* verb with the irregular **yo** form **pongo**, while **vestirse** is a stem-changing -*ir* verb.

4 The reflexive pronouns always come before the verb. If the verb is in the infinitive then the reflexive pronoun is joined onto the infinitive and needs to change according to whom you are referring to:

Quiero divertir**me** en la fiesta.   *I want to enjoy myself at the party.*
Mi amigo suele despertar**se** tarde.   *My friend usually wakes up late.*

¿Entiendes?

A Write out the following sentences filling the gaps with the correct reflexive pronoun chosen from the box.

me	te	se	nos	os	se

19

1 Y vosotros, ¿a qué hora ..... levantáis?

2 ¡Mis primos son unos golfos! ..... acuestan muy, muy tarde.

3 Mi madre ..... levanta bastante temprano.

4 Nosotros somos aguafiestas. No ..... divertimos nunca.

5 Yo no ..... ducho por la mañana, no hay tiempo.

6 ¿Qué ..... pones para ir al colegio?

B Now look at these pictures and complete the sentences to explain your daily routine.

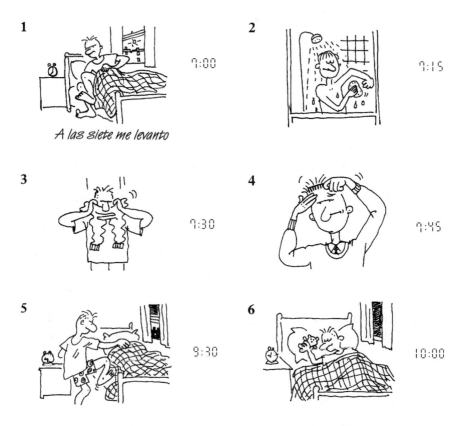

1

7:00

A las siete me levanto

2

7:15

3

7:30

4

7:45

5

9:30

6

10:00

Resumen

1 Reflexive verbs have **se** on the end of them in the infinitive:

lavarse	*to have a wash*
dormirse	*to sleep*

2 When we talk about different people the reflexive pronoun **se** on the infinitive changes depending on whom you are talking about, and goes before the verb. The verb that is left (ending in **ar**, **er** or **ir**) behaves as an **-ar**, **-er** or **-ir** verb. Be careful of irregular or stem-changing verbs.

yo	me	lavo	I wash	myself
tú	te	lavas	you wash	yourself
él/ella/Vd.	se	lava	he/she washes	himself/herself
			you wash	yourself
nosotros/as	nos	lavamos	we wash	ourselves
vosostros/as	os	laváis	you wash	yourselves
ellos/ellas/Vds	se	lavan	they wash	themselves
			you wash	yourselves

3 Reflexive verbs in the past and future tenses

Note that the reflexive pronouns stay the same in all the tenses. The three groups of verbs will follow the pattern of endings for each tense. Some are irregular or stem-changing:

Imperfect: Cuando iba al colegio **me** levantaba tarde cada día.
When I used to go to school, I used to get up late every day.

Perfect: Esta mañana **me** he lavado el pelo.
This morning I've washed my hair.

Preterite: Ayer por la tarde **me** acosté temprano.
Yesterday evening, I went to bed early.

Future: Este domingo **me** pondré el pantalón nuevo.
This Sunday I will put on my new trousers.

4 Infinitive

When the infinitive forms part of a sentence, the reflexive pronoun can be added to the end of the infinitive or placed before the other verb involved:

Me voy a comprar un coche nuevo./Voy a comprar**me** un coche nuevo.
I'm going to buy myself a new car.

8 Negatives

1 In simple terms a 'negative' means saying 'no' or refusing something. The simplest form of the negative in Spanish is to put **no** before the verb:

No tengo hermanos. *I haven't got any brothers.*
No soy tímido. *I'm not shy.*

2 There are several other negative expressions that you need to know:

no... nada *nothing*
no... nadie *no one, nobody*
no... nunca/jamás *never*
no... ni... ni... *neither ... nor*

When you use these expressions you can do so in two ways:

- The two negative words make a 'sandwich' around the verb, e.g.:

No tengo **nada** que decir. *I have nothing to say.*
No veo a **nadie** los fines de semana. *I see no one at weekends.*

- Before the verb or on its own, e.g.:

Nunca compro caramelos. *I never buy sweets.*
¿Vais mucho al campo? – **Nunca**. *Do you often go to the countryside? – Never.*

3 Some expressions you will need at the higher levels of the examination are:

no... ninguno *no, not any, none* (negative of **alguno**)
(**Ninguno** changes to **ningún** before a masculine singular noun. See Point 3.)
no... tampoco *not either, neither* (negative of **también**)

⚠️ **¡Atención!**

Note that very often two negative words are needed in Spanish. In English this is wrong but in Spanish it is grammatically correct and in fact is used very often and for emphasis, e.g.:

No me gusta **nada**. *(I don't like it at all.)*
Nunca he visto a **nadie** tan feo. *(I have never seen anyone so ugly.)*

¿Entiendes?

A Write out the following sentences filling in the gaps with the appropriate negative words.

1 ..... me gustan ..... los caramelos ..... los bombones.
2 ¡..... podré volver a correr!
3 ¿El inglés? ..... me gusta ...... Es aburrido.
4 ..... conocía a ..... en la fiesta.
5 ..... te bañes en el mar. Hay tormenta y es peligroso.
6 ..... tengo hermanos. Soy hijo único.
7 El año pasado fui a Estados Unidos, pero ..... volveré.

Resumen

1 The negative word goes before the verb.

2 If there are two negative words in the sentence (e.g. **no... nunca**) then they make a 'sandwich' around the verb.

3 The negative words in note 2 can be used on their own or before the verb in a sentence, but without the **no**.

9 Stem-changing verbs

1 Stem-changing verbs are a group of verbs that are also known as root-changing or radical-changing verbs. In simple terms this basically means that they have a change of spelling in the stem or main part of the verb.

You could say that they are irregular verbs, but they are only irregular in certain parts of the verb. Usually these changes only occur in the present tense, although not always so!

2 The stem-changing verbs can be divided into three groups:

A Verbs whose **e** changes to **ie**
Look at the example of how the verb **pref_e_rir** changes:

yo	prefiero
tú	prefieres
él/ella/Vd.	prefiere
nosotros	preferimos
vosotros	preferís
ellos/ellas/Vds.	prefieren

B Verbs whose **o** changes to **ue**
Look at the example of how the verb **v_o_lver** changes:

yo	vuelvo
tú	vuelves
él/ella/Vd.	vuelve
nosotros	volvemos
vosotros	volvéis
ellos/ellas/Vds.	vuelven

C Verbs whose **e** changes to an **i**
Look at the example of how the verb **p_e_dir** changes:

yo	pido
tú	pides
él/ella/Vd.	pide
nosotros	pedimos
vosotros	pedís
ellos/ellas/Vds.	piden

 **¡Atención!**

*You should have noticed that the **nosotros** and **vosotros** parts of the verb do not change in any of the patterns.*

D There are also verbs such as **nevar, llover, costar** and **doler**. All four verbs are stem-changing and have been put together here as they all exist in only one or two forms (singular and plural).

nevar ——▶ **nie**va *it snows*
llover ——▶ **llue**ve *it rains*

Examples
En las montañas de Escocia **nieva** mucho.
  In the mountains in Scotland it snows a lot.
En Inglaterra **llueve** mucho durante el verano.
  In England it rains a lot during the summer.

These two verbs only exist in the singular form. The other two verbs **costar** and **doler** you will probably see in two forms:

	singular	plural
costar ——▶	**cue**sta	**cue**stan
doler ——▶	**due**le	**due**len

Examples

El monedero **cuesta** mil pesetas.	*The purse costs 1000 pesetas.*
Hoy los plátanos **cuestan** doscientas el kilo.	*Today bananas cost 200 per kilo.*
¡Mamá! me **duele** mucho la cabeza.	*Mum, my head is aching a lot.*
También me **duelen** los ojos.	*My eyes are hurting too.*

3 There are of course some exceptions to consider:

A The verbs **dormir** and **morir** that change from **o** to **ue** in the present tense have an irregular spelling in the present participle (the 'ing' ending of the verb in English):
dormir (to sleep) ——▶ d**u**rmiendo (sleeping)
morir (to die) ——▶ m**u**riendo (dying)

B Another group of verbs carry the slight change in spelling into another tense.

The **-ir** verbs whose **e** changes to **i** in the **él/ella/Vd.** and **ellos/ellas/ Vds.** forms, also change their spelling in the same forms in the preterite tense. These verbs are:

reír	(to laugh)	⟶	rió	rieron
sentir	(to feel)	⟶	sintió	sintieron
servir	(to serve)	⟶	sirvió	sirvieron
sonreír	(to smile)	⟶	sonrió	sonrieron

They need to be learnt.

¿Entiendes?

A Draw up the following chart and see if you can fill in the missing items. Try to remember the rule about **nosotros** and **vosotros**. Some have been filled in for you.

	empezar *to begin*	tener *to have*	pensar *to think*	sentir *to feel*	sentarse *to sit down*	despertarse *to wake up*
yo	empiezo					
tú		tienes				
él/ella/Vd.			piensa			
nosotros				sentimos		
vosotros						
ellos/ellas/ Vds.						

	poder *to be able to*	mostrar *to show*	encontrar *to find*	probarse *to try on*	dormirse *to fall asleep*	moverse *to move*
yo	puedo					
tú		muestras				
él/ella/Vd.			encuentra			
nosotros				nos probamos		
vosotros						
ellos/ellas/ Vds.						se mueven

B In the box below are all the parts of the verbs **vestirse, elegir, repetir, servir** and **decir**. Put all the correct parts of each verb in order under its infinitive. The **yo** form of each verb has been done for you. Note the spelling of **elijo** where **j** replaces **g**.

Vestirse	Elegir	Repetir	Servir	Decir
me visto	elijo	repito	sirvo	digo

eliges	decimos	repetimos	repite	servís
sirven	nos vestimos	dicen	sirves	repiten
dices	elegimos	eligen	dice	decís
	te vistes	se viste	sirve	repetís
	os vestís	elige	servimos	repites
		elegís	se visten	

Resumen

1 Stem-changing verbs are called as such because a slight change in spelling in the stem or main part of the verb takes place when you go into the present tense from the infinitive. There are three main groups:

$$e \longrightarrow ie$$
$$o \longrightarrow ue$$
$$e \longrightarrow i$$

2 This change of spelling usually only occurs in the present tense. However, as usual, there are one or two exceptions (see note 3).

10 Commands

1 A command tells someone to do or not to do something, e.g.:

¡Siéntate!   *Sit down!*
¡No lo hagas!   *Don't do it!*

2 In Spanish four forms of the verb are used to give commands depending on whom you are talking to. These are known as imperatives. They correspond to the four different ways of expressing 'you' in Spanish:

Tú   *You* (singular; someone you know as a friend or relative)
Vosotros   *You* (plural; people you know as friends or relatives)
Vd.   *You* (singular, polite)
Vds.   *You* (plural, polite)

3 How to form *tú* and **vosotros** positive commands

A *Tú*   This is very similar to the *tú* form of the present tense, but without the **s**:

hablas ⟶ habla   ¡**Habla** con tu madre! *Speak to your mother!*
comes ⟶ come   ¡**Come** esas patatas! *Eat those potatoes!*
escribes ⟶ escribe   ¡**Escribe** la carta! *Write the letter!*

Notice the upside-down exclamation mark which comes before the imperative in Spanish as well as the normal one which follows it.

Some irregular verbs have an irregular form:
decir (to say, to tell)   ⟶ di
hacer (to do, to make)   ⟶ haz
ir (to go)   ⟶ ve
poner (to put)   ⟶ pon
salir (to go out, to leave) ⟶ sal
ser (to be)   ⟶ sé
tener (to have)   ⟶ ten
venir (to come)   ⟶ ven

B **Vosotros**   To form the **vosotros** imperative take the infinitive of the verb and change the *r* on the end to *d*:

```
hablar    ──►  hablad
comer     ──►  comed
escribir  ──►  escribid
```

4 How to form **Vd.** and **Vds.** positive commands

The part of the verb needed when you tell someone you address as
Vd. or **Vds.** to do something is the singular or plural part of the
present subjunctive (see Point 38):

```
hablar    ──►  hable (Vd.), hablen (Vds.)
comer     ──►  coma (Vd.), coman (Vds.)
escribir  ──►  escriba (Vd.), escriban (Vds.)
```

To form them all you have to do is take the **yo** form of the present
tense, take off the **o** and replace it with **e** or **en** for **-ar** verbs, and with
a or **an** for **-er** and **-ir** verbs:

Infinitive	Present	Imperative
mirar (to look)	miro (I look)	¡Mire Vd.!/¡Miren Vds.! (Look!)
beber (to drink)	bebo (I drink)	¡Beba Vd.!/¡Beban Vds.! (Drink!)
batir (to beat)	bato (I beat)	¡Bata Vd.!/¡Batan Vds.! (Beat!)

Some verbs which do not end in **o** in the **yo** form of the present tense
have irregular **Vd.** and **Vds.** imperatives:

Infinitive	Present	Imperative
dar (to give)	doy (I give)	¡Dé Vd.!/**Den** Vds.! (Give!)
estar (to be)	estoy (I am)	¡Esté Vd.!/**Estén** Vds.! (Be!)
ir (to go)	voy (I go)	¡Vaya Vd.!/¡Vayan Vds.! (Go!)
ser (to be)	soy (I am)	¡Sea Vd.!/¡Sean Vds.! (Be!)

Note also:

ver (to see)	veo (I see)	¡Vea Vd.!/¡Vean Vds.! (See!)

5 Negative commands are used to tell someone 'don't... !' **Tú, vosotros,**
Vd. and **Vds.** all use the present subjunctive form of the verb to give
negative commands (see Point 38).

	Hablar	Comer	Escribir
tú	no hables	no comas	no escribas
vosotros	no habléis	no comáis	no escribáis
Vd.	no hable	no coma	no escriba
Vds.	no hablen	no coman	no escriban

Remember that if a verb is stem-changing in the present tense then it will be in the imperative. Exceptions to this are **tenga** and **tengan** from **tener**, and **venga** and **vengan** from **venir**.

¿Entiendes?

A Match up the correct English sentence with the Spanish one:

1	¡Haz los deberes!	**a**	Come here!
2	¡Ven aquí!	**b**	Madam, come this way!
3	¡No lo hagas!	**c**	Sir, don't go in there!
4	Señora, ¡pase por aquí!	**d**	Do your homework!
5	Señor, ¡no entre allí!	**e**	Don't go out now!
6	¡No salgas ahora!	**f**	Don't do it!

B Write out the following recipe, filling in the gaps with the correct form of the verbs in brackets. Use the **Vd.** form of the imperative.

TORTILLA DE PATATAS

1 (Pelar) ..... y (cortar) ..... la cebolla en trozos

2 (Pelar) ..... y (cortar)..... las patatas en trozos

3 (Freír) ..... la cebolla y las patatas lentamente.

4 (Batir) .....
tres huevos en
un recipiente.

5 (Añadir) .....
las patatas y
la cebolla a los
huevos. (Poner)
..... un poco de
sal y pimienta.

6 (Cocinar) .....
a fuego lento
hasta que la
tortilla esté
dorada.

7 (Servir) ..... la
tortilla fría o
caliente con una
ensalada.

Resumen

1 A command tells someone to do or not to do something.

2 There are four forms of the verb according to whom you are talking to: **tú**, **vosotros**, **Vd.** and **Vds.**

3 Positive commands

Tú Take away **s** from present tense.
(See note 3 for irregular forms.)

Vosotros Take away **r** from infinitive and add **d**.

Vd./Vds. Take off the **o** of the **yo** form of the present tense, and replace it with **e** or **en** for **-ar** verbs, and with **a** or **an** for **-er** and **-ir** verbs (i.e. the forms of the present subjunctive – see Point 38 and the Verb Tables).
(See note 4 for irregular forms.)

4 Negative commands

No + **tú/Vd./vosotros/Vds.** forms of the present subjunctive

11 Ser and estar

1 In Spanish, there are two verbs meaning 'to be': **ser** and **estar**.

2 Uses of **ser**: the 'permanent' verb

- **Ser** is used when you are talking about professions and nationalities:
  Juan es médico.   *John is a doctor.*
  ¿Tú eres australiano?   *Are you Australian?*

- **Ser** is used when you are stating a fact that cannot change:
  Mi cumpleaños es el 15 de noviembre.
       My birthday is the 15th of November.
  Aquellas chicas son mis hermanas.   *Those girls are my sisters.*

- It is also used when you are talking about someone's personality or character:
  Mi padre es generoso.   *My father is generous.*
  La película es muy divertida.   *The film is very funny.*
  Ellas son buenas chicas.   *They are good girls.*

- **Ser** is almost always used for times, dates and numbers:
  Es la una y media.   *It's half past one.*
  Mañana es el día de Navidad.   *Tomorrow is Christmas Day.*
  ¿Cuánto es? – Son 500 pesetas.   *How much is it? – It's 500 pesetas.*

3 Uses of **estar**: the 'temporary' verb

- Estar is used when you are talking about the position or location of something or someone:
  El banco está al lado de correos.
       The bank is next to the post office.
  Londres está en el sur de Inglaterra.
       London is in the south of England.
  Manuel y yo estamos en casa.
       Manuel and I are at home.

- It is also used when the condition you are talking about is likely to, or expected to, change. This is usually with an adjective:
  María está contenta.   *María is happy.*
  Las camisas están limpias.   *The shirts are clean.*

¿Entiendes?

A Write out the following sentences filling in the gaps with the correct part of **ser** or **estar** in the present tense:

1 ¿Dónde ..... el banco?
2 ¡Hola! ¿Qué tal? ..... bien, gracias.
3 Hoy tú ..... muy deprimido.
4 Mi casa ..... bastante grande.

B Now write out the following and fill in the gaps with the correct part of **ser** or **estar** in the correct tense:

1 El año pasado mi hermano ..... muy egoísta. Ahora ..... más simpático.
2 ¿Y tú? ¿Dónde ..... anoche? Te busqué durante una hora.
3 El ladrón ..... pequeño y feo.
4 Hoy ..... triste, pero mañana ..... contenta. Es mi cumpleaños.

Resumen

1 **Ser** is used for: professions and nationalities
facts that cannot change
personality and character
times, dates and numbers

2 **Estar** is used for: position and location
conditions likely to change

● For all parts of **ser** and **estar** in all tenses see the Verb Tables.

12 The future tense

1 The future tense is used when you want to talk about an action or event that will happen some time in the future. There are two ways of expressing this: the 'immediate' future and the 'true' future.

2 We use the 'immediate' future in English when we want to say that something 'is going to' happen:

Esta noche **vamos a cenar** temprano.

> *Tonight we are going to have dinner early.*

Mañana **voy a visitar** Barcelona.

> *Tomorrow I am going to visit Barcelona.*

The 'immediate' future is made up of three parts:

> Present tense of the verb *ir* + *a* + infinitive

You will therefore need to know all the parts of the present tense of the verb *ir* (to go):

yo	**voy**	a	comer
tú	**vas**	a	beber
él/ella/Vd.	**va**	a	dormir
nosotros	**vamos**	a	leer
vosotros	**vais**	a	hablar
ellos/ellas/Vds.	**van**	a	andar

More examples
Yo **voy a empezar** el trabajo la semana que viene.

> *I am going to start work next week.*

Esta noche él **va a preparar** la cena.

> *Tonight he is going to prepare dinner.*

El próximo verano nosotros **vamos a ir** a Holanda.

> *Next summer we are going to go to Holland.*

3 We use the 'true' future in English when we want to say that something 'will' or 'shall' happen:

Iré a la universidad para estudiar ciencias.
I will go to University to study science.
Hablarán con los vecinos del problema.
They will talk to the neighbours about the problem.

The 'true' future is made up of two parts:

> The infinitive + the future endings

The future endings are the same for *-ar*, *-er* and *-ir* verbs. Look at the examples:

yo + infinitive + **é**	yo hablar**é**	*I will talk*
tú + infinitive + **ás**	tú comer**ás**	*you will eat*
él/ella + infinitive + **á**	él/ella beber**á**	*he/she will drink*
Vd. + infinitive + **á**	Vd. trabajar**á**	*you will work*
nosotros + infinitive + **emos**	nosotros ver**emos**	*we will see*
vosotros + infinitive + **éis**	vosotros ir**éis**	*you will go*
ellos/ellas + infinitive + **án**	ellos leer**án**	*they will read*
Vds. + infinitive + **án**	Vds. jugar**án**	*you will play*

Note that the **nosotros** ending **emos** is the only one that does not have an accent on it.

⚠ **¡Atención!**

Some verbs, however, do not behave as they should and are therefore irregular. The endings are the same, but the stem (the main part of the verb) changes slightly, and the future endings are then added to the stem. Examples:

decir	→ *diré*
hacer	→ *haré*
poder	→ *podré*
poner	→ *pondré*
querer	→ *querré*
saber	→ *sabré*
salir	→ *saldré*
tener	→ *tendré*
venir	→ *vendré*

¿Entiendes?

A Write out this letter filling in the gaps using the correct part of the verb **ir**:

Querida Juana,

¡Por fin yo ..... a ir a España! Yo ..... a estar en el aeropuerto de Barcelona el lunes, nueve de mayo. Mis padres ..... a llevarme al aeropuerto. Yo ..... a llegar sobre las doce del mediodía. ¿Qué ..... a hacer, tú y yo? ¿Nosotros ..... a ir a la discoteca? ¿Y tus padres? ¿Ellos ..... a estar de vacaciones? ¿Y tu hermano? ¿Qué ..... a hacer él? ¿Nosotros ..... a ir a algún sitio en especial? Por favor, escríbeme pronto.

Alison xxx

B Look at the horoscopes for these six star signs for next week. Write out the verbs in the future tense. Check your answers.

VIRGO   Ganarás mucho dinero en la lotería. ¡Buena suerte!

LIBRA   No será un día muy bueno. Tendrás muchos problemas.

ESCORPIÓN   En asuntos de amor no habrá ningún problema para ti.

SAGITARIO   Comprarás un coche nuevo o harás alguna compra grande.

CAPRICORNIO   En cuanto al trabajo, podrás mejorar tu posición esta semana.

ACUARIO   Esta semana tus problemas de dinero acabarán. Recibirás cierta cantidad de dinero.

C Now look at these predictions. Write them out filling in the gaps with a suitable verb in the future from the box opposite:

PISCIS   Esta semana ..... demasiado generoso. Ves con cuidado o no te ..... nada.

ARIES   Problemas con la familia ..... pronto. ..... que tener cuidado o te ....

TAURO   Cuidado con el coche esta semana. ..... algún problema con el motor. Arréglalo, o ..... el autobús.

36

GÉMINIS   Esta semana ..... lleno de emoción. Algo mágico te .....
¡Disfrútalo!
CÁNCER   ..... mucho esta semana. ..... descansar un poco o te .....
demasiado.
LEO   ..... de excursión dentro de poco y ..... en avión.

serás	irás	tendrás	necesitarás
habrá	cogerás	trabajarás	quedará
empezarán	viajarás	cansarás	
estarás	pasará	enfadarás	

Resumen

Future tense

1 *Ir* + *a* + infinitive for plans and immediate future

2 Infinitive + future endings for any occasion in the future

13 A, al, a la, a los, a las

1 **A** on its own means 'to':

Voy a Francia.   *I am going to France.*
Voy a estudiar.   *I am going to study.*

It applies to towns, cities and countries with no exceptions, and can also be followed by an infinitive (see Point 12).

2 When you are going to a place, like the café, disco or shops, the expression you use (**al, a la, a los, a las**) depends on whether the place you are going to is masculine or feminine, singular or plural.

- masculine singular, e.g. el banco:
  Voy **al** banco. (a + el = al)

- feminine singular, e.g. la discoteca:
  Voy **a la** discoteca.

- masculine plural, e.g. Los Juegos Olímpicos:
  Voy **a los** Juegos Olímpicos.

- feminine plural, e.g. las tiendas:
  Voy **a las** tiendas.

3 Given that **a** means 'to' and **el/la/los/las** mean 'the', the following all mean 'to the': **al/a la/a los/a las**.

¿Entiendes?

A Write down this list of places. In front of each place write down whether you should use **al, a la, a los, a las**, or just **a** on its own.

1	..... camping	6	..... España
2	..... comisaría	7	..... cines
3	..... tienda de deporte	8	..... bibliotecas
4	..... carnicería	9	..... parques
5	..... colegio	10	..... supermercado

Resumen

A means *to*.
Al (masculine singular) means *to the*.
A la (feminine singular) means *to the*.
A los (masculine plural) means *to the*.
A las (feminine plural) means *to the*.

14 De, del, de la, de los, de las

1 De can mean several things:

A It can mean 'about':
El libro es de espías.   *The book is about spies.*

B It can mean 'from':
Soy de Cáceres.   *I'm from Cáceres.*
Han llegado de Chile.   *They have arrived from Chile.*

C It can mean 'of' (indicating that something belongs to someone):
Es el padre de Miguel.   *He is the father of Michael./*
                          He's Michael's father.
El dinero es de Juan.   *It's Juan's money./It's the money of Juan.*

⚠️ **¡Atención!**

There is no equivalent of 's in Spanish.

D De can also mean 'of' (indicating what something is made of).
Es de oro.   *It's made of gold.*
Es de algodón.   *It's made of cotton.*

2 Del, de la, de los, de las
Given that **de** means 'of' or 'from' and that **el, la, los** and **las** all mean 'the', **del, de la, de los, de las** all mean 'of/from the'. They are used when you want to say 'of the' or 'from the' but which one you use depends on whether the object that follows is masculine or feminine, singular or plural.

- masculine singular (**del**)
  las llaves **del** hotel   *the keys of the hotel*
  Viene humo **del** motor.   *There's smoke coming from the engine.*

- feminine singular (**de la**)
  el dueño **de la** frutería   *the owner of the fruiterer's*
  el bolsillo **de la** camisa   *the pocket of the shirt*

- masculine plural (**de los**)
  los uniformes **de los** alumnos　　*the uniforms of the pupils*
  La respuesta vino **de los** directores.　*The answer came from the managers.*

- feminine plural (**de las**)
  el color **de las** rosas　　*the colour of the roses*
  el vuelo **de las** aves　　*the flight of the birds*

¿Entiendes?

A Follow the example given as a guide and write out a sentence using each group of words given:

Example
la madre/mi amiga es/Barcelona
La madre de mi amiga es de Barcelona.

1　el dinero es/familia
2　los coches/trabajadores son/empresa
3　la casa/vecinos/es más grande que la casa/Pedro
4　yo soy/Madrid, pero mis padres son/provincia de Gerona
5　mi reloj es/oro

Resumen

1 **De** means 'about', 'from', or 'of' (expressing belonging or what something is made of).

2 **Del, de la, de los, de las** all mean 'of the' or 'from the'.

	masculine	**feminine**	
singular	del	de la	of/from the
plural	de los	de las	of/from the

15 Prepositions

1 A preposition is a word that indicates a link or relationship between things or people. It can, for example, tell you where something is:

El banco está **enfrente del** hotel.   *The bank is facing the hotel.*

Can you match up the Spanish on the left with the English on the right?

1	cerca de	**a**	in front of
2	lejos de	**b**	next to
3	enfrente de	**c**	facing
4	delante de	**d**	near to
5	detrás de	**e**	far from
6	al lado de	**f**	behind

Check your answers in the Resumen.

2 You will notice that all the above expressions in Spanish end in **de**. The **de** has to change to **del**, **de la**, etc, according to the place that follows it (see Point 14):

enfrente de (+ el banco) = enfrente **del** banco
cerca de (+ la catedral) = cerca **de la** catedral
lejos de (+ los hoteles) = lejos **de los** hoteles
delante de (+ las tiendas) = delante **de las** tiendas

3 Some prepositions (**de, a, para, por, con** and **sin**) are used with a verb. In such cases you need to write the verb that follows in the form of the infinitive:

Lo hace para **ganar** dinero.   *He is doing it to earn money.*
Salió sin **decir** adiós.   *She left without saying goodbye.*

4 Some verbs take a specific preposition to make a phrase, e.g. **hablar con** (to speak to/with), **empezar a** (to begin to), **acabar de** (to have just), etc:

Empezaron **a** cantar.   *They began to sing.*
Acabo **de** telefonearle.   *I have just phoned him.*

¿Entiendes?

A Look at the map of the town. Write out the sentences below it filling in the gaps with **del, de la, de los** or **de las**.

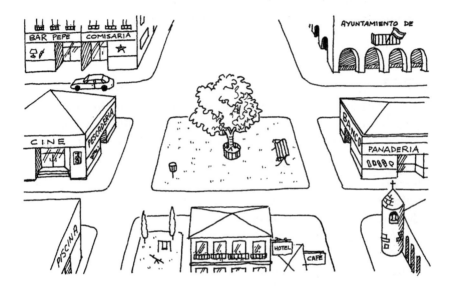

1 El hotel está al lado ..... cafetería.
2 El parque está al lado ..... hotel.
3 La pescadería está enfrente ..... banco.
4 El coche está cerca ..... comisaría.
5 La iglesia está enfrente ..... panadería.

B Now complete the expressions with the correct prepositions, including **del, de la,** etc.

1 La pescadería está ..... banco.
2 La comisaría está ..... bar.
3 La panadería está ..... iglesia.
4 El parque está ..... hotel.
5 La piscina está ..... parque.

⚠ ¡Atención!

Note that you will see words indicating location like **cerca**, **lejos**, **detrás**, etc. used without **de**. In such cases they are no longer prepositions but adverbs of place (see Point 4). Look at these examples:

El cine está muy **cerca**. *(The cinema is very near.)*
La playa no está muy **lejos**. *(The beach isn't very far.)*
La casa está ahí **detrás**. *(The house is behind there.)*
Mi amigo está allí **enfrente**. *(My friend is over there.)*

Resumen

1 A preposition is a word that indicates a link or relationship between things or people. Many prepositions tell you where something or someone is in relation to something or someone else:

cerca de	*near (to)*
lejos de	*far from*
enfrente de	*facing*
delante de	*in front of*
detrás de	*behind*
al lado de	*next to*
dentro de	*inside, in*
fuera de	*outside*
debajo de	*underneath*
en	*in, on*
sobre	*on*
encima de	*on top of, over, above*

2 If **de** forms part of the preposition it may have to change to **del**, **de la**, **de los**, **de las**, depending on what comes after it (see Point 14):

cerca de María	*near María*
cerca del bar	*near the bar*
cerca de la piscina	*near the swimming pool*
cerca de los hoteles	*near the hotels*
cerca de las tiendas	*near the shops*

16 Conjunctions

1 A conjunction is a word that you use to join up two sentences or clauses.

Can you match the correct English word with the Spanish?

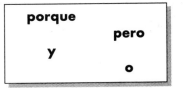

porque

pero

y

o

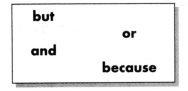

but

or

and

because

Check your answers in the Resumen.

2 Note these odd spelling changes:

Y, meaning 'and', changes to **e** when followed by a word beginning with **i** or **hi** (because the two similar 'i' sounds are not easy to pronounce together):
Compré peras **e** higos.   *I bought pears and figs.*

O, meaning 'or', changes to **u** when followed by a word beginning with **o** (because the two similar 'o' sounds are not easy to pronounce together):
Necesito unos siete **u** ocho.   *I need about seven or eight.*

¿Entiendes?

A Rewrite the sentences using a suitable word from the box below to link each pair together.

1 Mi hermano es simpático. Es travieso.
2 Estudio ciencias. Me gustan mucho.
3 Mañana vamos al cine. A lo mejor a la discoteca.
4 Voy a comprar un nuevo compact disc. Mi amiga también.

o   pero   porque   y

B Write out these sentences filling the gaps with **y, e, o** or **u**.

1 Mi hermana es guapa ..... inteligente.
2 No sé si ir al cine con Nuria ..... Amanda.
3 Empiezo el trabajo en verano ..... otoño.
4 Mi primo ..... yo vamos a la discoteca el sábado.
5 Seguiré estudiando francés ..... inglés.

Resumen

1 Conjunctions: words that join up two sentences or clauses.

2 porque   *because*
   pero   *but*
   y   *and*
   o   *or*

3 Remember:

   y ⟶ e (when followed by an i or hi)
   o ⟶ u (when followed by an o or ho)

17 The personal *a*

When you are talking about an action that is happening to a particular person (e.g.: phoning them, seeing them, visiting them, etc.) and the person is the direct object of the verb, you need to put an **a** between the verb and that person:

Examples

Vi **a** tu padre.	*I saw your father.*
Mi hermano visita **a** mis abuelos.	*My brother visits my grandparents.*
¿Conoces **a** mi hermana?	*Do you know my sister?*
Golpeó **al** árbitro.	*He punched the referee.*

¿Entiendes?

A Five of the following phrases need **a** in front of the person. Five do not. Write out the sentences putting in the personal **a** where you think it is needed.

1 Los alumnos visitan ..... su profesor.
2 Las chicas quieren hablar con ..... sus novios.
3 Tengo que ver ..... mi abuela.
4 Me gusta la música clásica. Admiro mucho ..... Mozart.
5 Vi ..... un gato en la calle.
6 Anoche leí ..... un libro de aventuras.
7 Voy a ayudar ..... mi amiga.
8 Escribí ..... una carta.
9 Me gusta mucho ..... mi perro. Es travieso.
10 Oye Juan, ¿conoces ..... mi prima Ana?

Resumen

The personal **a** must be used when the direct object of the action of a verb is a particular person. The **a** always goes before that person.

Vamos a visitar **a** tu tío.
No conoce **a** mis padres.
Mañana veré **a** mi profesor de música.

18 Possessives

1 Adjectives ('my', 'your', 'his', 'her', 'its', 'our', 'their')

A In English we use the words 'my', 'your', 'his', etc. when we want to talk about whom things belong to.

B In Spanish, there are two words meaning 'my': **mi** and **mis**.
Mi is used when you talk about a singular noun (masculine or feminine): **mi coche** (my car), **mi casa** (my house).
Mis is used when you talk about a plural noun (masculine or feminine): **mis libros** (my books), **mis llaves** (my keys).

C Just like **mi** and **mis**, there are singular and plural forms for 'your', 'his', 'her', 'its' and 'their'. Look at the table that follows and you will see that with just two exceptions the possessive adjectives all follow this pattern: singular and plural (NOT masculine and feminine).

my	mi/mis	our	nuestro/nuestros (masc.)
your	tu/tus		nuestra/nuestras (fem.)
his	su/sus	your	vuestro/vuestros (masc.)
her	su/sus		vuestra/vuestras (fem.)
its	su/sus	their	su/sus
your	su/sus	your	su/sus
(Vd. polite)		(Vds. polite)	

Which two are the exception to the rule? Why?
Nuestro and **vuestro** have four forms: masculine singular and plural, and feminine singular and plural.

2 Pronouns ('mine', 'yours', 'his', 'hers', 'its', 'ours', 'theirs')

A There are also several words in Spanish to replace 'mine', 'yours', etc.

Can you match up the Spanish and the English in the following lists:

1	mío	a	yours
2	tuyo	b	ours
3	nuestro	c	mine
4	suyo	d	theirs
5	vuestro	e	yours
6	suyo	f	his/hers/its/yours

Check your answers in the Resumen.

Be careful. **Nuestro** and **vuestro** are the same as the possessive adjectives (note 1). However **mío, tuyo** and **suyo** are normally used on their own.

For example, the question **¿De quién es el libro?** (Whose is the book?) could be answered in two ways:

Es mi libro. (It's my book.) OR **Es mío.** (It's mine.)

B All six words have four versions: masculine singular and plural, feminine singular and plural, as you can see in the table.

masculine singular	feminine singular	masculine plural	feminine plural
(el) mío	(la) mía	(los) míos	(las) mías
(el) tuyo	(la) tuya	(los) tuyos	(las) tuyas
(el) suyo	(la) suya	(los) suyos	(las) suyas
(el) nuestro	(la) nuestra	(los) nuestros	(las) nuestras
(el) vuestro	(la) vuestra	(los) vuestros	(las) vuestras
(el) suyo	(la) suya	(los) suyos	(las) suyas

Examples

¿Este libro es tuyo?	*Is this book yours?*
No, no es mío; es suyo.	*No, it isn't mine; it's his/hers.*
¿Estas llaves son tuyas?	*Are these keys yours?*
No, las mías están en la mesa.	*No, mine are on the table.*
Juan tiene su pasaporte pero he olvidado el mío.	*Juan has his passport but I have forgotten mine.*

Notice that the definite article (**el, la, los, las**) is not used with these forms when they follow any part of **ser** (to be).

¿Entiendes?

A Ana is writing about her family. Write out the passage and fill in the gaps for her using the words in the box.

49

¡Hola!, me llamo Ana y tengo 15 años. Hay seis personas en .....
familia: ..... padre, ... madre, ... dos hermanos, y ..... hermana.
También hay ..... perro, que se llama Boby. ..... padre es alto. .....
pelo es negro. ..... madre se llama Juana y es simpática. .....
hermanos se llaman Ricardo y Alberto. Son tontos. ..... hermana
se llama María y tiene novio. ..... novio se llama Andrés. Tenemos
un coche. ..... coche es azul y es muy rápido. ¿Y tú? ¿Cómo es .....
familia? ¿Tenéis coche? ¿De qué color es ..... coche?

mi	mi	tu	mis	su	nuestro
vuestro	mi	mi	su	mis	
nuestro	mi	mi	mi		

B Put the following sentences into Spanish and fill in the puzzle. Numbers 1
and 9 are examples and have been done for you:

1 My car
2 Our house
3 Your dog (singular)
4 His garden
5 Your sisters (plural)
6 My parents

7 Your brother (singular)
8 Their sweets
9 (The house?) It's theirs
10 (The cars) are yours
11 (The cat) is mine
12 (The keys) are mine

50

Resumen

1 Possessive adjectives

masculine singular	feminine singular	masculine plural	feminine plural	English
mi	mi	mis	mis	my
tu	tu	tus	tus	your
su	su	sus	sus	his her its your
nuestro	nuestra	nuestros	nuestras	our
vuestro	vuestra	vuestros	vuestras	your
su	su	sus	sus	their your

2 Possessive pronouns

masculine singular	feminine singular	masculine plural	feminine plural	English
(el) mío	(la) mía	(los) míos	(las) mías	mine
(el) tuyo	(la) tuya	(los) tuyos	(las) tuyas	yours
(el) suyo	(la) suya	(los) suyos	(las) suyas	his hers its yours
(el) nuestro	(la) nuestra	(los) nuestros	(las) nuestras	ours
(el) vuestro	(la) vuestra	(los) vuestros	(las) vuestras	yours
(el) suyo	(la) suya	(los) suyos	(las) suyas	theirs yours

19 The preterite tense

1 The preterite tense is the English equivalent of the simple past, e.g. 'I went', 'I saw', 'I visited', etc. It is used to describe a single, completed action in the past.

2 You form the preterite tense in Spanish by taking the **ar, er** or **ir** ending off the infinitive of the verb, and adding on the preterite endings to the stem.

Look at these examples and note the endings:

Habl**ar**	Com**er**	Viv**ir**
habl**é**	com**í**	viv**í**
habl**aste**	com**iste**	viv**iste**
habl**ó**	com**ió**	viv**ió**
habl**amos**	com**imos**	viv**imos**
habl**asteis**	com**isteis**	viv**isteis**
habl**aron**	com**ieron**	viv**ieron**

You will notice that there are only two sets of endings to learn as **-er** and **-ir** verbs share the same endings.

3 Unfortunately, some of the most frequently used verbs in Spanish are irregular in the preterite tense. Because you use the verbs a lot you tend to remember them easily.

Look at the **yo** form of some irregular verbs. Can you match them up with the infinitives? Which two verbs are the same in the preterite tense? Check your answers.

1 dar	**a** hice
2 estar	**b** fui
3 hacer	**c** puse
4 ir	**d** di
5 poner	**e** fui
6 ser	**f** vine
7 tener	**g** estuve
8 venir	**h** tuve

For all parts of verbs in the preterite tense, see the Verb Tables.

A Choose the correct verb in the preterite tense that fits in with the meaning of the sentence. Write out each sentence and underline the verb. The first one has been done for you.

1 Ayer (<u>visité</u>, comí) el castillo.
2 Mi perro (bebió, comió) un hueso.
3 Las chicas (tuvieron, vieron) el concierto.
4 El verano pasado (trabajé, fui) a Tenerife.
5 Anoche (llegué, fui) con mi amigo a la discoteca.
6 Mi madre (vendió, compró) una falda nueva.

B Luisa has written a postcard to a friend from her holidays. Write it out, filling in the gaps with one of the words from the box below.

Hotel Sol, Mallorca

Querida Marta,

     ¡Estoy en Mallorca! ¡Qué fantástico todo! Ayer ..... sol durante todo el día y ..... todos a la playa. Yo ..... el día en la arena. De vez en cuando ..... el sol y ..... en el mar. ¡Qué maravilla!
Luego, por la noche, mi amiga y yo ..... a la discoteca y ..... a dos chicos americanos. ¡Qué guapos! ¡Te veré pronto y te lo contaré todo!

Un abrazo

Luisa

---

pasé	me bañé	hizo	conocimos	fuimos
	fuimos	tomé		

Resumen

1 The Spanish preterite tense is the equivalent of the English simple past ('I did', 'I played', etc.)

2 The endings to be learnt are:

-ar verbs	-er/-ir verbs
é	í
aste	iste
ó	ió
amos	imos
asteis	isteis
aron	ieron

3 Some of the most common verbs are irregular (**dar, estar, hacer, ir, poder, poner, ser, tener, venir**). Learn them!

20 The perfect tense

1 The perfect tense is used to talk about an action in the past which is completed or finished, i.e. something that has happened.
Look at the examples and work out the difference between using the perfect tense and the preterite tense:

Perfect tense

He preparado la comida.	*I have prepared lunch.*
He tomado cereales para desayunar.	*I have had cereal for breakfast.*
He leído la carta.	*I have read the letter.*

Preterite tense

Preparé la comida.	*I prepared lunch.*
Tomé cereales para desayunar.	*I had cereal for breakfast.*
Leí la carta.	*I read the letter.*

The perfect tense in Spanish is used in the same way as the perfect tense in English; to talk about something you have done (e.g.: 'I have been') whereas the preterite tense is used when you use the simple past in English: (e.g.: 'I went').

2 The perfect tense is formed in the following way:

Haber	+	*Past participle*
(The present tense of **haber** indicates who has done the action. It is known as the auxiliary verb, as it helps the main verb. It conveys the 'have' or 'has'.)		(This is the part of the main verb which indicates which action took place, e.g. 'been', 'gone', 'spoken', 'eaten', etc.)

3 You will need to know all the parts of the verb **haber** in the present tense:

yo	he
tú	has
él/ella/Vd.	ha
nosotros/as	hemos
vosotros/as	habéis
ellos/ellas/Vds.	han

Note that you do not use **tener** to form the perfect tense. The formation of the past participle of regular verbs follows a pattern:

-ar verbs   Take off the **ar** and add **ado**:
hablar ⟶ hablado.

-er and **-ir** verbs   Take off the **er** or **ir** and add **ido**:
comer ⟶ comido.
vivir ⟶ vivido.

 **¡Atención!**

- *Note that the construction* **he hablado, has comido,** *etc. cannot be separated in a sentence.*

- *If the sentence is in the negative form, the* **no** *goes before both parts of the perfect tense:*
  No *he vivido* **nunca** *en España. (I have never lived in Spain.)*

4 Sometimes you can use the perfect tense to give a reason for something that has happened:

Me duele la cabeza porque he bebido demasiado.
I have a headache because I have drunk too much.
No me encuentro bien porque he comido algo malo.
I don't feel well because I've eaten something bad.

¿Entiendes?

A Fill in the puzzle opposite putting the phrases in English into Spanish. Look at the example that has been filled in for you.

1 I have visited.
2 You (tú) have eaten.
3 We have bought.
4 They have danced.

5 You (Vd.) have gone down.
6 You (vosotros) have had.
7 She has played.
8 He has asked.

56

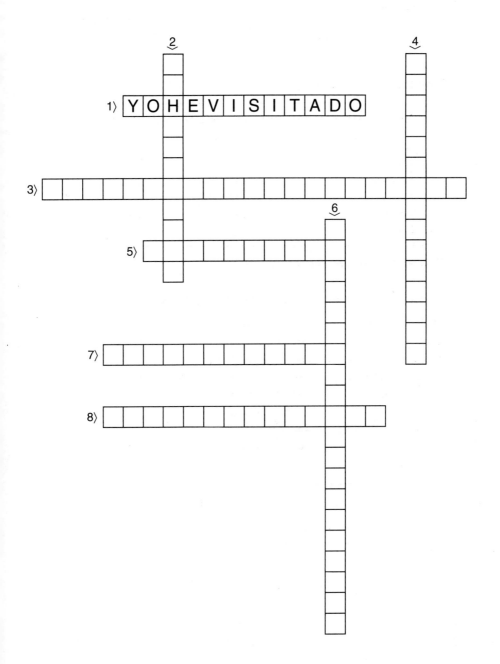

1) Y O H E V I S I T A D O

Resumen

1. The perfect tense is used for completed actions in the past. It is used when in English we would use 'has' or 'have' 'visited/been/written', etc.

2. The construction is easy:

Present tense of auxiliary verb **haber** + past participle	
he	comido
has	dormido
ha	hablado
hemos	cerrado
habéis	bebido
han	ganado

Remember that **tener** is not used.

3. A few common verbs have irregular past participles:

abrir (*to open*) ⟶ abierto (*opened*)
decir (*to say*) ⟶ dicho (*said*)
escribir (*to write*) ⟶ escrito (*written*)
hacer (*to do/make*) ⟶ hecho (*done/made*)
morir (*to die*) ⟶ muerto (*died*)
poner (*to put*) ⟶ puesto (*put*)
romper (*to break*) ⟶ roto (*broken*)
ver (*to see*) ⟶ visto (*seen*)
volver (*to return*) ⟶ vuelto (*returned*)

21 The imperfect tense

1 The imperfect tense is used on three different occasions:

A To describe an action that used to happen regularly in the past:
Los domingos **visitaba** a mi abuela.
> *On Sundays I used to visit (I would visit) my grandmother.*

B To describe an action that was happening in the past but not completed. It is often used to set the scene:

Ella **iba** a casa.   *She was going home.*
Ellos **comían** perritos calientes.   *They were eating hot dogs.*

Note how the imperfect differs from the preterite tense (Point 19) which often describes a sequence of events in the past:

Ella **iba** a casa cuando la **vi**.   *She was going home when I saw her.*
Ellos **comían** cuando **telefoneó**.   *They were eating when she phoned.*

C To describe certain things in the past (in preparation for the higher parts of the GCSE exam).

Remember $\boxed{\text{P P C H W F}}$. This stands for:
People   Places   Clothes   Hair   Weather   Feelings

Examples

Era feo.	*He was ugly.*
Era un sitio bonito.	*It was a pretty place.*
Llevaba una camisa azul.	*She was wearing a blue shirt.*
Tenía los ojos verdes.	*She had green eyes.*
Hacía sol.	*It was sunny.*
Estaba contenta.	*I was happy.*

2 To form the imperfect tense you take off the **ar**, **er**, and **ir** endings of the infinitives and add on the imperfect endings. Look at the verbs set out here and note the endings in these examples:

Hab**lar**	Com**er**	Viv**ir**
habl**aba**	com**ía**	viv**ía**
habl**abas**	com**ías**	viv**ías**
habl**aba**	com**ía**	viv**ía**
habl**ábamos**	com**íamos**	viv**íamos**
habl**abais**	com**íais**	viv**íais**
habl**aban**	com**ían**	viv**ían**

You should notice two things:

A Once again there are only two sets of endings to learn, as **-er** and **-ir** share the same endings.

B There is an accent on the first **i** of all the endings of the **-er** and **-ir** verbs, and on the first **a** of the **nosotros** form of **-ar** verbs.

3 Radical changing verbs and irregular verbs form the imperfect tense as shown above (that is regularly):

costar   ⟶   cost**aba**, cost**abas**, cost**aba**, cost**ábamos**, cost**abais**, cost**aban**

ped**ir**   ⟶   ped**ía**, ped**ías**, ped**ía**, ped**íamos**, ped**íais**, ped**ían**

ten**er**   ⟶   ten**ía**, ten**ías**, etc.

quer**er**   ⟶   quer**ía**, quer**ías**, etc.

4 There are three exceptions: **ser**, **ir** and **ver**:

Ser	Ir	Ver
era	iba	veía
eras	ibas	veías
era	iba	veía
éramos	íbamos	veíamos
erais	ibais	veíais
eran	iban	veían

¿Entiendes?

A Match up the sentences correctly. Those on the left describe what used to happen when Pedro was seven; those on the right describe what happens now.

Cuando tenía 7 años

1 Jugaba en la calle con los amigos.

2 Bebía mucha Coca-Cola.

Ahora

a ¡Me encantan!

b Trabajo todo el día y no estudio.

3 Mis padres me daban 1000 pesetas a la semana.

4 Mi hermana y yo nos peleábamos cada día.

5 Estudiaba mucho en el cole.

6 No me gustaban las chicas.

c Somos buenos amigos Angela y yo.

d Voy a la discoteca con mis amigos.

e Prefiero la cerveza.

f ¡No me dan nada!

B Look at the picture. You were at the scene of the crime. You are a vital witness for the police. Using the verbs on the left and the vocabulary on the right, can you write a description of what happened using the imperfect tense?

Verbs	Vocabulary
llevar	coche saco dinero pelo oscuro
ir	rizado corto gafas tejanos zapatillas
correr	largo rubio falda camiseta moderno blanco
salir	limpio grande pequeño

61

Resumen

1 The imperfect is used to describe:
- what used to happen (regularly) in the past
- what was happening in the past
- particular things in the past (P P C H W F)

2 The **ar, er** and **ir** endings are taken off the infinitive and the following endings are added:

-ar	-er/-ir
aba	ía
abas	ías
aba	ía
ábamos	íamos
abais	íais
aban	ían

3 **Ser, ir** and **ver** are totally irregular!

22 Making questions

1 All questions in Spanish have two question marks around them. An upside down question mark at the beginning of the question and a 'normal' one at the end: **¿Cómo te llamas?**

2 A question can be made from a sentence just by changing the intonation of your voice at the end of the sentence. Try saying these four phrases as normal, then as questions. (Your voice should go up at the end for a question!) Check your answers with a friend.

Hay bocadillos de jamón.
Se puede aparcar delante de la tienda.
El museo está abierto mañana.
El desayuno está incluido.

Match up the question words in Spanish with the English. Note that all the question words in Spanish have an accent:

1 ¿Cuánto?	**a** What?
2 ¿Qué?	**b** Who?
3 ¿Cuál?	**c** When?
4 ¿Cuándo?	**d** Why?
5 ¿Dónde?	**e** How much?
6 ¿Por qué?	**f** Which?
7 ¿Cómo?	**g** How many?
8 ¿Quién?	**h** What/How?
9 ¿Cuántos?	**i** Where?

See Resumen for answers.

3 **¿Qué?**, **¿Cuándo?**, **¿Dónde?**, **¿Cómo?** and **¿Por qué?** never change.

● **¿Cuál?** and **¿Quién?** have two forms:
  singular: ¿Cuál? ¿Quién?
  plural: ¿Cuales? ¿Quiénes?

● **¿Cuánto?** has four forms:
  masculine singular: ¿Cuánto? ⟶ ¿Cuánto dinero tienes?
  masculine plural: ¿Cuántos? ⟶ ¿Cuántos amigos tienes?
  feminine singular: ¿Cuánta? ⟶ ¿Cuánta gente había?
  feminine plural: ¿Cuántas? ⟶ ¿Cuántas casas tienes?

4 Some question words are used in combination with a preposition:

¿De qué está hecho tu bolso?   *What is your bag made of?*

The **qué** question word has another word in front of it, the preposition **de** meaning 'from' or 'of'. We will refer to this as an extended question word.

Notice the position of the extended question word in Spanish. Both parts are together at the begining of the question, with the original question word in second position. Compare it with the English, where the original question word, such as 'what' or 'who', goes at the beginning of the question and the extra word at the end of the sentence:

¿Con quién vas al teatro?   ***Who(m)*** *are you going to the theatre* ***with?***

Years ago you would have said in English: 'With whom are you going to the theatre?' The English has changed but the Spanish has not!

¿Entiendes?

A Write out these questions filling in the gaps with the correct question word.

1 ¿ ..... años tienes?
2 ¿ ..... se llama tu hermano?
3 ¿ ..... es tu cumpleaños?
4 ¿ ..... es tu número de teléfono?
5 ¿ ..... estudias español? Porque me encanta.
6 ¿ ..... vives ahora?
7 ¿ ..... te gusta más? ¿El azul o el verde?
8 ¿ ..... es tu profesor preferido en el colegio?
9 ¿ ..... tiempo necesitas para ir a tu casa?
10 ¿ ..... es tu perro?

B Match up the sentences on the left with the sentences on the right.

1 ¿Adónde vas?   **a** What is this dish made of?
2 ¿En qué consiste este plato?   **b** Where have you come from?
3 ¿De quién es este bolso?   **c** When do you want the notes for?
4 ¿De qué está hecho este   **d** Where are you going (to)?
  pastel?

5 ¿A qué hora cenamos?

6 ¿Para quién compras el abanico?

7 ¿A quién te presento?

8 ¿De dónde has venido?

9 ¿Con quién irás a Tenerife?

10 ¿A cuál de las dos chicas te refieres?

11 ¿Para cuándo quieres los apuntes?

12 ¿Hasta cuándo estarás allí?

e Which of the two girls are you referring to?

f When will you be there until?

g What is this cake made of?

h Who(m) does this bag belong to?

i Who(m) will you go to Tenerife with?

j Who(m) are you buying the fan for?

k What time are we having dinner (at)?

l Who(m) shall I introduce you to?

Resumen

1 A question needs two question marks round it (¿ ... ?).

2 A question can be made by making your voice go up at the end of a sentence.

3 All question words have an accent on them to show that they are questions.

4 Important question words (Note also the extended questions in exercise B of ¿Entiendes?):

¿Cuánto?	*How much?*
¿Cuántos?	*How many?*
¿Qué?	*What?*
¿Cuál?	*Which?*
¿Cuándo?	*When?*
¿Dónde?	*Where?*
¿Adónde?	*Where (to)?*
¿Por qué?	*Why?*
¿Cómo?	*How?/What?*
¿Quién?	*Who?*

23 Por and para

1 **Por** and **para** can both mean 'for'. However there are certain differences. **Por** often means 'by', 'through' or 'because of'; **para** often means 'to', or 'in order to'.

2 **Por** is used:

A to mean 'through':
Pasamos **por** la ciudad.   *We passed through the city.*
El ladrón entró **por** la ventana.   *The thief entered through the window.*

B to mean 'on behalf of':
Lo hago **por** mi madre.   *I'm doing it for my mother.*

C to mean 'because of', 'in support of':
Voy al trabajo **por** el dinero.   *I go to work because of the money.*
Le quiero **por** su personalidad.   *I love him because of his personality.*
Estoy **por** la protección del   *I'm for the protection of the*
   medio ambiente.   *environment.*

D to express 'by' with a passive verb:
Este libro fue escrito **por** mi profesora de español.
    This book was written by my Spanish teacher.

E to mean 'in exchange for':
Me pidió demasiado dinero **por** su coche.
    He asked me too much money for his car.

F with the verb **ir** to mean 'to get':
Voy al supermercado **por** patatas.
    I'm going to the supermarket to get some potatoes/for some potatoes.

G with measurements meaning 'per':
Condujo a ochenta kilómetros **por** hora.
    He drove at eighty kilometres per hour.

H with parts of the day:
por la mañana   *in the morning*
por la tarde   *in the afternoon/evening*
por la noche   *in the/at night*

I with time:
Me esperó **por** media hora.   *He waited for me for half an hour.*

3 *Para* is used:

A to express destination or intention:

Este tren va **para** Barcelona.   *This train goes to Barcelona.*

Mañana, mi hermano sale **para**   *Tomorrow, my brother goes to the*
la Universidad.   *University.*

Estas flores son **para** ti.   *These flowers are for you.*

B to express purpose or use:

Este cuaderno sirve **para** apuntar vocabulario nuevo.

                This notebook is used to note new vocabulary.

C in expressions of time:

- 'by' a certain time:

   Mi hermana estará lista **para** las nueve.

            My sister will be ready by nine.

- for a particular time:

   Tengo que estar en el dentista **para** las diez.

            I have to be at the dentist's at ten o'clock.

D in answer to *¿para qué?* meaning 'what for?' You usually answer this using

para   + infinitive ('to', 'in order to')

OR

para que + subjunctive ('so that', 'in order that')

Estudio mucho **para conseguir** un buen empleo.

            I study hard (in order) to get a good job.

¡Préstame el dinero **para que pague** la multa!

            Lend me the money so that I can pay the fine!

¿Entiendes?

A Look at the sentences in English and decide whether you would use **por** or **para** in Spanish. Check your answers:

1 I love him for his money.
2 Is this the bus for the station?
3 This new coat is for him.

4 You've got to be at the pool for 10 o'clock.
5 In the evening, I go to my friend's house.
6 I'm working to get some money.
7 My homework was corrected by my teacher.
8 I play squash to keep fit.
9 I am for animal rights.
10 This present is for you.

Resumen

Before you use 'for' in English think of its meaning:

- Does it mean 'for a purpose', 'destined for', 'intended for'? If so, use **para**.

- Does it mean 'through', 'in support of', 'on behalf of', 'because of', 'in exchange for'? If so, use **por**.

24 The pluperfect tense

1 You use the pluperfect tense when you want to talk about what had happened. It is used to explain completed actions in the past but at a point further back in time than the perfect tense (see Point 20). Very often it was the first thing to happen in the chain of events.

Perfect
He ido a España.　　*I've been to Spain.*

Pluperfect
Había ido a España.　　*I had been to Spain.*

2 The formation of the pluperfect is similar to the perfect tense, but this time the verb **haber** is used in the imperfect form, thus:

Imperfect of **haber**		+	past participle
yo	había		visitado
tú	habías		ido
él/ella/Vd.	había	+	comido
nosotros/as	habíamos		hablado
vosotros/as	habíais		estado
ellos/ellas/Vds.	habían		salido

¿Entiendes?

A Look at these sentences in English. For each one write down whether you would need to use the perfect (p) or pluperfect (pl) tense. Then, put the sentence into Spanish. Check your answers!

1 Have you been to Spain?
2 I had already seen the film.
3 She had waited for her father.
4 We had taken the boat.
5 Has he had good marks?
6 He had finished his homework.
7 I have visited Barcelona.
8 They have eaten all the apples.

Resumen

The pluperfect is formed in a similar way to the perfect tense (Point 20) but uses the imperfect of **haber** with the past participle. Remember that the pluperfect is one step further back in time than the perfect tense.

To form the pluperfect:

Imperfect of auxiliary verb **haber**	+ past participle
había	comido
habías	dormido
había	hablado
habíamos	cerrado
habíais	bebido
habían	ganado

25 The present and imperfect continuous

1 The present continuous

This tense is used to describe something that is happening NOW, THIS MINUTE. It is easily identified in English as the main verb ends in 'ing'. This is called the 'present participle', and has a Spanish equivalent which is simple to form:

-ar verbs: Take off **ar** and add **ando**
               hablar ———➤ hablando (speaking)

-er/-ir verbs: Take off **er/ir** and add **iendo**
               comer ———➤ comiendo (eating)
               vivir   ———➤ viviendo (living)

For irregular present participles see the Verb Tables.

The verb needed with this construction is the present tense of **estar** (to be) thus:

Present tense of **estar**		+	present participle
yo	estoy		cantando
tú	estás		hablando
él/ella/Vd.	está	+	estudiando
nosotros/as	estamos		comiendo
vosotros/as	estáis		bebiendo
ellos/ellas/Vds.	están		saliendo

Examples
Manuel **está bebiendo** agua.   *Manuel is drinking water.*
Ana y Marta **están viendo**   *Ana and Marta are watching*
   la televisión.   *television.*

2 The imperfect continuous

Just as we have learnt how to say that something *is* happening now by using the present continuous tense, we can also learn how to say that something *was* happening at the very moment that you were talking or writing about it by using the imperfect continuous.

The construction of the imperfect continuous is similar to the present continuous, except that the verb **estar** is in the imperfect tense. The present participle stays the same.

Thus:

Imperfect tense of **estar**		+	present participle
yo	estaba		cantando
tú	estabas		hablando
él/ella/Vd.	estaba	+	estudiando
nosotros/as	estábamos		comiendo
vosotros/as	estabais		bebiendo
ellos/ellas/Vds.	estaban		saliendo

¿Entiendes?

A Describe the following pictures using the present continuous. The first example has been done for you:

1 *Él está bailando.*

2

3

4

5

6

7

8

B Write at least five sentences about this picture. Use the imperfect continuous and the verbs given to help you.

beber	comer	charlar	bailar	divertirse
	escuchar	mirar		

Example
En la fiesta los chicos estaban mirando a las chicas.

Resumen

1 You use the present continuous to describe what is happening NOW:
Jorge está comiendo chocolate.   *George is eating chocolate.*

> Present tense of **estar** + present participle (**-ando**, **-iendo**)

2 You use the imperfect continuous to describe what WAS happening at the very time of speaking or writing.
Jorge estaba comiendo chocolate. *George was eating chocolate.*

> Imperfect tense of **estar** + present participle (**-ando**, **-iendo**)

26 Pronouns and their positions

1 A pronoun is a word that replaces an object, thing or person (i.e. a noun). It is often used to avoid the repetition of that particular noun.

2 The pronouns used to replace objects are:

Noun	Pronoun
masculine singular	lo
feminine singular	la
masculine plural	los
feminine plural	las

Look at how these pronouns are used and where they go in a sentence:

Juan, ¿tienes el dinero?.	*Juan, have you got your money?*
Sí, **lo** tengo.	*Yes, I've got it.*
Ana, ¿compraste la falda?.	*Ana, did you buy the skirt?*
Sí, **la** compré.	*Yes, I bought it.*
Raquel, ¿dónde tienes tus pendientes?	*Raquel, where do you keep your earrings?*
Los tengo en mi bolso.	*I keep them in my bag.*
No encuentro mis llaves.	*I can't find my keys.*
Yo tampoco **las** encuentro.	*I can't find them either.*

You should have noticed that the pronoun comes before the verb.

3 The pronouns used to replace people are:

me = *me, to me*	**nos** = *us, to us*
te = *you, to you*	**os** = *you, to you* (plural)
lo = *him, you* (masc.)*	**los** = *them, you*** (masc.)
le = *him, to him, to her* *you, to you** (masc.)	**les** = *them, to them* (masc.) *you, to you*** (masc.)
la = *her, you* (fem.)* *you, to you** (fem.)	**las** = *them, to them*** (fem.) *you, to you*** (fem.)

* These are used for the **Vd**. polite form.
** These are used for the **Vds**. polite form.
Lo and *los* are used mainly in Latin America.

Examples

Mi padre **me** compró un nuevo coche.	*My father bought me a new car.*
Le visité en su casa.	*I visited him at home.*
Les regalé unos caramelos.	*I gave them some sweets as a present.*
Os di dinero para Navidad.	*I gave you money for Christmas.*

Note that these pronouns can be both the direct object of or the indirect object of a verb:

Direct object

Te vi en la playa.	*I saw you on the beach.*

Indirect object

¿**Te** dio el dinero?	*Did he give you the money?/ Did he give the money to you?*

4 When two object pronouns come together in a sentence the first person pronouns (**me** and **nos**) will come before any other one:

Me lo prestó.	*He lent it to me.*

In the same way the second person pronouns (**te** and **os**) precede a third person one:

¿**Te lo** dio?	*Did he give it to you?*

When two third person pronouns come together the indirect ones (**le, la, les, las**) come before the direct ones (**lo, la, le, los, las, les**). They also change to **se**:

Se lo di.	*I gave it to him.* (instead of **le lo** di)
Se las dieron.	*They gave them to them.* (instead of **les las** dieron)

5 Position of pronouns in different tenses

Tense	Example	Position
Present	**Lo** tengo **La** compro	Before verb
Preterite	**Lo** tuve **La** compré	Before verb
Future	**Lo** tendré **La** compraré	Before verb

Table – *continued*

Tense	Example	Position
Imperfect	**Me** adoraba **Le** gustaba	Before verb
Imperfect continuous	**Lo** estaba buscando Estaba buscándo**lo**	Before **estar** or attached to the end of the present participle
Present continuous	**La** está poniendo Está poniéndo**la**	Before **estar** or attached to the end of the present participle
Perfect	**Lo** he vendido **La** he roto	Before verb
Pluperfect	**Le** había dado **Lo** había comido	Before verb
Subjunctive	Quiero que **lo** cojas	Before verb
Infinitive	**Lo** tenemos que ver Tenemos que ver**lo**	Before the first verb or on the end of the infinitive

6 In a negative sentence the pronoun will come between **no** and the verb:

Antonio no **lo** quiere.	*Anthony doesn't want it.*
No **lo** hizo.	*He didn't do it.*
No **lo** voy a comer.	*I'm not going to eat it.*
No **la** está bebiendo.	*She isn't drinking it.*

In the last two examples the pronoun could also be placed on the end of the infinitive or present participle:

No voy a comer**lo**.
No está bebiéndo**la**. (Note the accent added to the second **e**; it would also be added to the **a** in an **-ar** verb: **Está mirándola**.)

7 In commands the pronoun is attached to the end of the command form (imperative) of the verb:

¡Hazlo!/¡Hágalo!   *Do it!*
¡Dámelo!/¡Démelo!   *Give it to me!*

If the command is a negative one, the pronoun is placed after **no** and before the verb:

¡No **lo** hagas!/¡No **lo** haga!   *Don't do it!*
¡No **me lo** des!/No **me** lo dé!   *Don't give it to me!*

 ¡Atención!

*These object pronouns are not used after prepositions. The pronouns you have to use then are: **mí** (me), **ti** (you), **él** (him), **ella** (her), **Vd.** (you), **sí** (himself, herself, yourself, themselves, yourselves), **nosotros/as** (us), **vosotros/as** (you), **ellos/ellas** (them), **Vds.** (you):*

¿Para quién es el regalo? (Who is the present for?)
*Es para **mí**. (It's for me.)*
*Lo compré para **él**. (I bought it for him.)*
*Lo compró para **sí**. (He bought it for himself.)*

*When **mí, ti** and **sí** are used with **con** (with) they form one word as follows: **conmigo, contigo, consigo** to mean 'with me', 'with you', 'with him/her/you'.*

¿Entiendes?

A You have just spent two weeks in Spain with your pen-friend and her mother helps you to pack your case. Answer the questions using the pronouns **lo, la, los** or **las**. The first example has been done for you. ¡Suerte!

Ana,   ¿Tienes tu falda? Sí, la tengo.
  ¿Tienes tus calcetines rojos?
  ¿Tienes tus tejanos?
  ¿Y tu jersey amarillo?
  ¿Tienes tus gafas de sol?
  ¿Llevas tu camiseta azul?
  ¿Tienes todos tus regalos?
  ¿Cogiste tu pasaporte y dinero?

B Choose from the pronouns below to fill in the gaps.

1 He told me it. .... dijo.
2 I bought you them. .... compré.
3 I gave it to her. .... di.
4 I was telling them. ..... estaba diciendo.
5 They had given us them. .... habían dado.
6 We took it to you (plural). .... llevamos.

me	lo	te	les	los	se
lo	os	los	lo	nos	

Resumen

1 Pronouns replace an object or person to avoid repetition of the same thing several times.

2 Pronouns to replace objects: *lo, la, los, las*.

3 Pronouns to replace people: *me, te, lo, le, la* (singular)
                                              nos, os, los, les, las (plural).

4 Pronouns normally come before the verb. They can, however, be attached to the end of an infinitive or present participle. They are always attached to the end of a positive command.

27 The conditional tense

1 You use the conditional tense in Spanish when you want to say that something 'should', 'would' or 'could' be done:

Debería hacer mis deberes.   *I should do my homework.*
Los chicos dijeron que no   *The boys said that they wouldn't go to*
   irían a la playa.   *the beach.*

2 The conditional tense is formed in a similar way to the 'true' future tense (see Point 12). The infinitive is used as a stem and the future endings are replaced by the imperfect endings (see Point 21):

yo	com**ería**	*I should/would eat*
tú	com**erías**	*you should/would eat, etc.*
él/ella/Vd.	com**ería**	
nosostros/as	com**eríamos**	
vosotros/as	com**eríais**	
ellos/ellas/Vds	com**erían**	

 **¡Atención!**

Where a verb is irregular in the future tense, it is also irregular in the conditional:

tener – tendría, tendrías, etc.
poder – podría, podrías, etc.

The conditional form of **querer** *is* **querría, querrías, etc.** *However, because it is so similar to the imperfect form* **quería,** *it is usually replaced by* **quisiera** *(I would like) which is in fact an imperfect subjunctive (see Point 38).*

Note that there is one set of endings for all verbs, **-ar**, **-er** *and* **-ir**.

¿Entiendes?

A Write down the verbs in this passage which are in the conditional.

Ayer fui al médico porque me encontraba muy mal. Me dolía la garganta y todo el cuerpo. El médico me dio algunos consejos: 'Si yo fuese tú' dijo, 'iría a mi casa inmediatamente. Me tomaría dos aspirinas y me metería en la cama en seguida. Descansaría durante una semana y no saldría de la casa – Tienes la gripe. Yo bebería mucho y comería bien. No haría nada.' Entonces yo volví a casa y como buen paciente hice todo lo que me dijo el médico.

Resumen

1 The conditional is formed in a similar way to the 'true' future. (If a verb is irregular in the future tense it will be in the conditional.)

Infinitives	-ar	Endings	ía
			ías
	-er		ía
			íamos
	-ir		íais
			ían

- Same endings for the three groups of infinitive.

2 Remember **quisiera** (I would like).

28 Expressions with tener

1 The verb **tener** on its own means 'to have'. When it is used in certain expressions it can mean 'to be':

Tengo hambre.   *I am hungry.*
Mi madre tiene 48 años.   *My mother is 48 years old.*

2 The only part of these expressions to change is **tener**, which changes according to who is referred to.
(See the Verb Tables for **tener** in all tenses.)

3 These expressions can be useful when you do the higher part of the examination because they enable you to explain how you feel. Describing your feelings in the past requires the imperfect tense (see Point 21 for a reminder).

4 You could also describe how you will feel, using the future tense (see Point 12). But be careful! **Tener** has an irregular future stem! (See the Verb Tables.)

¿Entiendes?

A Can you work out the meaning of the following expressions? Use the pictures to help you. Check your answers in the Resumen.

1 Tener frío   2 Tener hambre   3 Tener miedo (de)

4 Tener prisa

5 Tener... años

6 Tener calor

7 Tener sed

8 Tener suerte

9 Tener ganas (de)

B Put the following sentences into Spanish.

1 I was hungry.
2 He is cold.
3 You (tú) are lucky.
4 We are 18 years old.
5 You (vosotros) two were thirsty last night.
6 They will be in a hurry tomorrow.
7 I feel like going out.
8 My father is afraid of spiders.

Resumen

Tener used in the following expressions means 'to be':

tener frío	*to be cold*
tener calor	*to be hot*
tener hambre	*to be hungry*
tener sed	*to be thirsty*
tener miedo (de)	*to be afraid (of)*
tener suerte	*to be lucky*
tener prisa	*to be in a hurry*
tener... años	*to be ... years old*
tener ganas (de)	*to be in the mood for (to feel like)*

29 Comparatives and superlatives

1 Comparatives

A When you want to compare two or more different things, you can use several expressions. Look at the pictures, and see if you can work out what the phrases mean, and the three different ways of comparing things:

Jorge es **más** inteligente **que** Pedro y Antonio.
Pedro es **menos** inteligente **que** Antonio.
Antonio no es **tan** inteligente **como** Jorge.

What do these expressions mean?

más... que
menos... que
tan... como

Check your answers in the Resumen.

B You will notice that all three expressions are 'sandwiched' around the adjective that is used to make the comparisons:

España es **más** grande **que** Suiza.   *Spain is bigger than Switzerland.*

C Other expressions to use for comparing things are:

tanto/a... como   *as/so much as ...*
tantos/as... como   *as/so many as ...*

Examples
No tengo **tanto** chocolate   *I haven't got as much chocolate as*
   como tú.   *you.*
No tiene **tantos** libros   *He hasn't got as many books as*
   como discos.   *records.*

83

2 Superlatives

A When you want to say that something is the most important or the biggest or the best in some way you can use: **el más** (masculine) or **la más** (feminine) before the adjective:

Mi hermana es **la más** guapa. *My sister is the prettiest.*
Mi perro es **el más** tonto. *My dog is the stupidest.*

B They can be used in the plural too – **los más** (masculine) or **las más** (feminine):

Tus primos son **los más** altos. *Your cousins are the tallest.*
Esas casas son **las más** feas. *Those houses are the ugliest.*

C When you want to say that something is the best in the class/world, etc., you use **de** to mean 'in' (not **en**):

Esta chica es la más bonita **del** mundo. *This girl is the prettiest in the world.*

Enrique es el más inteligente **de** la clase. *Henry is the most intelligent in the class.*

● **Exceptions**
Unfortunately, in both cases there are of course exceptions!

Adjective	Comparative	Superlative
bueno/a (good)	mejor (better)	el/la mejor (the best)
malo/a (bad)	peor (worse)	el/la peor (the worst)

Mejor and **peor** do not have separate feminine forms, only singular and plural.

Éstas son las **mejores** zapatillas de deporte que tengo. *These are the best trainers I've got.*

Es la **peor** casa del pueblo. *It's the worst house in the village.*

¿Entiendes?

A ¿Verdadero o Falso?

1 Pepe

2 Andrés

19 años

17 años

3 Nacho

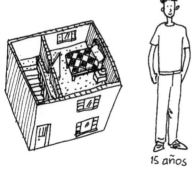

15 años

1 Nacho es más alto que Andrés.
2 Pepe es el más viejo.
3 Andrés es más joven que Nacho.
4 La casa de Nacho no es tan grande como la casa de Pepe.
5 En la casa de Andrés no hay tantas habitaciones como en la casa de Pepe.
6 Andrés es el más grande.

B **Europa**

Write out the following sentences filling in the spaces with a suitable phrase in the comparative or superlative form.

1 España es ..... grande ..... Inglaterra.
2 Inglaterra no es ..... pequeño ..... Suiza.
3 Bélgica tiene ..... islas ..... Grecia.
4 Rusia es el país ..... grande ..... todos.
5 España no tiene ..... ríos ..... Noruega.
6 Suiza es el país ..... montañoso.

Resumen

1 Comparing things

Use the following expressions 'sandwiched' around the adjective:

más... que	*more ... than*
menos... que	*less ... than*
tan... como	*as/so ... as*
tanto/a... como	*as/so much ... as*
tantos/as... como	*as/so many ... as*

- **Más... de** also means 'more ... than', but is only used with numbers and quantities:

  Tengo más **de** un kilo de naranjas.
  I've got more than one kilo of oranges.

  Hay más **de** veinticinco personas en mi clase.
  There are more than 25 people in my class.

2 To say that something is 'the most' or the '-est' (e.g. 'biggest'), you put the following in front of the adjective:

el más
la más
los más
las más

3 Don't forget the exceptions:

bueno/a ⟶ mejor ⟶ el/la mejor
buenos/as ⟶ mejores ⟶ los/las mejores
malo/a ⟶ peor ⟶ el/la peor
malos/as ⟶ peores ⟶ los/las peores

30 Expressions using *lo*

1 **Lo** literally means 'it' and can sometimes change its meaning according to the sentence.

2 You can use **lo** with an adjective:

lo bueno   *the good thing*
lo malo   *the bad thing*

A See if you can work out what the following expressions mean. Write them down with the English meaning next to them.

B When you have done that put a (+) next to the positive statements and a (-) next to the negative ones. Look at the example:

1 lo importante   *the important thing (+)*
2 lo peor
3 lo aburrido
4 lo mejor
5 lo interesante
6 lo fácil
7 lo difícil

3 Note that you can use this construction followed by **de** or **es que**:

Lo mejor de España son las playas.   *The best thing about Spain are the beaches.*
Lo peor es que siempre hace mucho calor. *The worst thing is that it is always hot.*

4 **Lo** + **que** can mean 'that', 'which' or 'what':

Todo lo que tengo.   *All that I have.*
Lo que significa...   *Which means ...*
Lo que importa...   *What matters ...*

5 Other useful expressions:

No lo sé.   *I don't know.*
No lo entiendo. *I don't understand it.*

31 Expressions using *tener que*, *hay que*, *acabar de* and *deber*

1 *Tener que*, *hay que* (coming from **haber que**) and **deber (de)** all express the idea of 'having to' or 'must'.

Tener que is the strongest, most forceful expression.
Hay que is the next.
Deber (de) is the weakest, least forceful expression.

2 Tener que

You will need to know all the parts of the verb **tener** (see Verb Tables). The verb following **tener que** is in the infinitive:
Tengo que ir mañana.   *I have to go tomorrow.*

3 Hay que

This expression comes from **haber** (the verb used to form the perfect and pluperfect tenses) and means 'one has to ...'.
It is followed by an infinitive:
Hay que rellenar este formulario.   *You must fill in this form.*

4 Deber (de)

- **Deber** is a regular **-er** verb. It is followed by another verb in the infinitive when it has the meaning 'must':
Debo comer verdura.   *I must eat greens.*
No debes hablar con su novia.   *You must not talk to his girlfriend.*

- When **deber** is followed by **de** before an infinitive it means 'must' in the sense of an assumption you are making:
Debe de ser Teresa.   *It must be Teresa.*

5 Acabar de

- **Acabar** is a regular **-ar** verb meaning 'to finish'. When it is used in the present tense and is followed by **de** and an infinitive it has the meaning of 'to have just' done something:
Yo acabo de terminar los   *I have just finished my*
  deberes.   *homework.*
Juan acaba de llegar.   *John has just arrived.*

Note that you do not use the perfect tense (Point 20) to convey the meaning of 'have just'.

- By putting the verb *acabar* into the imperfect tense, you can transform 'have just' one step further back in the past to 'had just'. This means that you do not use the pluperfect tense (Point 24) for 'had just':

| Acabábamos de salir del cine. | *We had just come out of the cinema.* |

¡Atención!

All four expressions are followed by the infinitive form of the verb.

¿Entiendes?

A Match up the part of the sentence on the left with the correct part on the right:

1 Yo	**a** debemos comportarnos bien
2 Oye, una cosa,	**b** tienes que ver a tu sobrina
3 Usted	**c** hay que terminarlo pronto
4 Lara y Agustín	**d** acabo de terminar los deberes
5 Tú	**e** acaban de casarse. ¡Enhorabuena!
6 Nosotros	**f** debe pasar delante

Resumen

1 *Tener que, hay que, deber (de)*
All three of them mean 'to have to do' something.

2 *Acabar de* means 'to have just done' something.

3 All the above are followed by another verb in the infinitive, and are useful verbs to know for higher parts of the GCSE examination.

32 Impersonal verbs: expressing likes, dislikes and opinions

1 There are certain expressions you can use when you want to say what you like and dislike.

Match the following symbols with the correct expression to indicate how much you like something: **✗, ✔, ✔✔, ✔✔✔**.

me gusta(n) mucho
me gusta(n)
me encanta(n)
no me gusta(n)

Check your answers.

2 How to use **gustar** and **encantar**

A You will see that the verbs **gustar** and **encantar** are used in the following forms:
me gusta and **me gustan**; **me encanta** and **me encantan**.

B These two verbs are unusual for two reasons:

● **Me gusta** literally means 'it pleases me'. There is no equivalent in Spanish of the English phrase 'I like'.

● They are only used in the third person forms, depending on whether the thing you like or dislike is singular (**me gusta**) or plural (**me gustan**).
Therefore you use **gusta** or **gustan** according to whether the thing that is being liked or disliked is singular or plural. The person who does the liking or disliking is indicated by the appropriate object pronoun (**me, te, le, nos, os, les**):

me gusta(n)	*I like*	nos gusta(n)	*we like*
te gusta(n)	*you like*	os gusta(n)	*you like*
le gusta(n)	*he, she, it likes*	les gusta	*they like*
	you (Vd.) like		*you (Vds.) like*

Examples

Me gusta el café.	*I like coffee.*
Me gustan los animales.	*I like animals.*
¿Les gusta la música?	*Do they like music?*
No **le gustan** las manzanas.	*He doesn't like apples.*

c You cannot use the subject pronouns (***yo, tú, él, etc.***) with these verbs. If you want to emphasise the person who is involved you have to use ***a mí, a ti, a él, a ella, a Vd., a nosotros, a vosotros, a ellos, a ellas*** or ***a Vds.***, as follows:

a mí, me gusta(n)	a nosotros, nos gusta(n)
a ti, te gusta(n)	a vosotros, os gusta(n)
a él, le gusta(n)	a ellos, les gusta(n)
a ella, le gusta(n)	a ellas, les gusta(n)
a Vd., le gusta(n)	a Vds., les gusta(n)

You can also use ***a*** followed by the name of the person concerned.

Examples

A mí, me gusta el fútbol.	*I like football.*
¿**A ella,** le gusta el fútbol?	*Does she like football?*
A mi hermano, le gusta el chocolate.	*My brother likes chocolate.*
A ellos, les gustan las naranjas.	*They like oranges.*
A Martín, no le gusta el pescado.	*Martin doesn't like fish.*

D You can emphasise whether you like something or not by using ***me gusta(n) mucho*** (I really like/I like very much) and ***no me gusta(n) nada*** (I really don't like/I hate):

Me gustan mucho los caballos.	*I really like horses.*
No me gusta nada la historia.	*I hate history.*

E Note: You use the verb ***encantar*** in the same way as ***gustar*** with the sense of 'to love':

Les encanta la música.	*They love music.*
Me encantan estos zapatos.	*I love these shoes.*

¿Entiendes?

A Match up the two halves of the sentences so that they make sense. Write out the complete sentences.

1 No me gusta el tenis,	**a** los tomates.
2 A Enrique	**b** ¿te gusta la playa?
3 No me gustan	**c** ¡les gustan los chicos!
4 ¡Oye! ¡Vosotros!	**d** no nos gustan los deberes
5 ¿Y a ti?	**e** no le gusta el fútbol
6 A mis hermanos y a mí	**f** ¿os gusta el colegio?

| 7 A Marisol y a Luis | g prefiero el baloncesto |
| 8 A las chicas | h les encantan las hamburguesas |

Check your answers.

B Now translate these sentences into Spanish.

1 María loves museums.
2 We love Spanish.
3 They hate homework.
4 My friends love the disco.
5 I really like chocolate.
6 My brother doesn't like studying.

 **¡Atención!**

Note that the following verbs also follow the same pattern as **gustar** and **encantar**:

Verb	English	Example
interesar	*to be interested in*	*Me interesa la política.*
entusiasmar	*to be keen on*	*Me entusiasma el baile.*
apetecer	*to fancy something*	*Me apetece una bebida fresca.*
doler	*to hurt/be painful*	*Me duele la cabeza.*
parecer	*to seem (to be)*	*¿Te parece una buena idea?*
hacer falta	*to need*	*Le hace falta un nuevo pantalón.*

Resumen

1 When you use **gustar** or **encantar** with an object (e.g. **el museo, las hamburguesas**) you always need to include the word for 'the' (**el, la, los, las**).

2 **Gusta(n)** and **encanta(n)** depend on the object being singular or plural. You can use a verb after **gustar** or **encantar** but it must be in the infinitive:

Me encanta bailar flamenco. *I love dancing flamenco.*

Note: The infinitive in Spanish is often translated by the '-ing' form in English.

3 Remember: **Gusta** and **gustan** agree with what is being liked or disliked. **Me, te**, etc. agree with who does the liking or disliking.

33 Soler and poder

1 **Soler** is a stem-changing verb (**o** to **ue**) meaning 'to be accustomed to', 'to be used to'. It can also be translated as 'usually':

Suelo coger el tren para ir al trabajo.	*I usually take the train to get to work.*
Ellos **suelen** jugar al tenis los viernes.	*They usually play tennis on Fridays.*

Used in the imperfect tense **soler** is translated as 'used to':

Solía ir al cine los sábados.	*He used to go to the cinema on Saturdays.*

2 **Poder** is also a stem-changing verb (**o** to **ue**). It means 'to be able to', 'can':

¿**Puedo** entrar?	*Can I go in?*
Él **puede** ir solo.	*He can go by himself.*

3 Both **soler** and **poder** can be used in another way. You can put **se** in front of the **él/ella/Vd.** part of the verb to mean 'one' or 'people/you' in general:

Se suele tomar aspirinas para curar el dolor de cabeza.	*You usually take aspirin to cure a headache.*
Cuando llueve, **se suele** llevar paraguas.	*When it rains you usually take an umbrella.*

Se puede ir en avión a Inglaterra.	*You can go to England by plane.*
¿**Se puede** comer aquí?	*Can we (one) eat here?*

● Note that both **soler** and **poder** are followed by the infinitive of the verb.

¿Entiendes?

A Match up the two halves of the sentences so that they make sense. Write out the complete sentences, then translate them into English.

1 Suelo jugar	**a** a España
2 Se puede comprar	**b** la televisión por las tardes
3 Solían ir de vacaciones	**c** con Ana
4 No puede ir	**d** queso en el supermercado
5 ¿Suele mirar... ?	**e** los lunes
6 ¿Se puede cambiar... ?	**f** al fútbol los sábados
7 ¿Puedo hablar... ?	**g** dinero en este banco
8 Suele acostarse temprano	**h** al cine mañana

34 Conocer and saber

1 Both of these verbs mean 'to know'.

2 Conocer means to know a person or a place:

¿Conoces Madrid?   *Do you know Madrid?*
¿Conoces a mis padres?   *Do you know my parents?*

3 Saber means to know a fact or how to do something:

¿Sabes bailar?   *Can you dance?*
¿Sabes a qué hora llega el tren?   *Do you know what time the train arrives?*

4 Conocer and **saber** are irregular verbs (see the Verb Tables).

¿Entiendes?

A Write out the sentences filling in the gap with the correct part of **conocer** or **saber**.

1 Ayer ..... a los padres de mi novio.
2 ¡Yo no ..... qué hacer con mi pelo!
3 Yo no ..... Barcelona, pero ..... que es una ciudad muy bonita.
4 El año pasado yo no ..... tocar la flauta.
5 Nosotros no ..... a nuestro profesor nuevo, pero ..... que es muy bueno.

Resumen

- **Conocer** = to know (people or places)
- **Saber** = to know (facts or how to do something)

35 Weather expressions

1 There are three main verbs used to describe the weather: **hacer, estar** and **haber (hay)**.

Match up each of these expressions with the appropriate picture of the weather:

está nublado	**hace sol**	**está lloviendo**	**hay niebla**
hace mal tiempo	**hace calor**	**está nevando**	
hace buen tiempo	**hay tormenta**	**está despejado**	
	hace viento	**hace frío**	

1

2

3

4

5

6

7

8

9

10

11

12

2 In higher parts of the GCSE examination, you will need to be able to use the three verbs **estar, hacer** and **haber** in the imperfect tense to describe what the weather was like.

You might also need to use the preterite tense to describe what the weather was like at a determined point in time, and the future tense to understand what the weather will be like from a weather forecast.

Look at the table below to help you see how the verbs change:

Infinitive	Present	Future	Preterite	Imperfect
hacer	hace	hará	hizo	hacía
estar	está	estará	estuvo	estaba
haber	hay	habrá	hubo	había

3 Other verbs you might need to use are **nevar** (to snow), with a stem change from **e** to **ie** (**nieva**), and **llover** (to rain), with a stem change from **o** to **ue** (**llueve**):

En Escocia nieva en las montañas.	*In Scotland it snows in the mountains.*
Nevaba en enero.	*It used to snow in January.*
Estaba nevando cuando llegué.	*It was snowing when I arrived.*
En Inglaterra llueve mucho.	*In England it rains a lot.*
Llovía durante el invierno.	*It used to rain in the winter.*
Estaba lloviendo cuando salió.	*It was raining when he went out.*

4 Note too these expressions:

Llueve a cántaros.	*It's raining cats and dogs.*
Hace un día de perros.	*It's a really awful day.*
Hace un frío que pela.	*It's freezing cold.*

¿Entiendes?

A Look at the letter that Marta sent to her friend describing her holiday. Choose an appropriate verb from the box below the letter to fill in each gap and write out the letter. Be careful! Some are in the imperfect, some in the preterite and some in the present tense.

Blanes
Costa Brava

Querida Paula,

¡Hola! ¿Qué tal? Yo bien. Bueno, ... aquí en Blanes y me lo ..... bomba! El martes ..... a la playa con un chico que ..... el lunes. ..... guapísimo!. Se ..... Norse y ..... de Noruega. Él ..... que allí ..... mucho frío en invierno. Casi siempre ..... nevando y ..... ir a esquiar a las montañas. ¡Te ..... una foto de Norse! Pues aquí la semana pasada el tiempo ..... fatal. ..... lloviendo a cántaros y ..... un frío que ...... ¿Y allí? ¿Qué .....hace? Nos vemos pronto,

Marta

estoy	**paso**	**suele**	**fui**	**fue**
conocí	**es**	**viene**	**pela**	**dice**
está	**hace**	**tiempo**	**llama**	
hacía	**estaba**	**enseñaré**		

Resumen

Three verbs are used with the weather:

hacer:
hace sol	*it's sunny*
hace calor	*it's hot*
hace frío	*it's cold*
hace viento	*it's windy*
hace mal/buen día	*the weather is bad/fine*
hace mal/buen tiempo	*the weather is bad/fine*

estar:
está granizando	*it's hailing*
está nevando	*it's snowing*
está despejado	*it's clear*
está nublado	*it's cloudy*
está lloviendo	*it's raining*

haber:
hay lluvia	*it's raining*
hay niebla	*it's foggy*
hay tormenta	*it's stormy*
hay escarcha	*it's frosty*

36 Numbers

1 Cardinal numbers are the ordinary, everyday numbers that we all use: one, two, three, etc. In Spanish they follow a fairly straightforward pattern that is quite easy to learn.

Here is a list of the numbers. Read the notes explaining the pattern carefully.

A Tens and units

● 1–10
You will certainly need to learn these unit numbers as a basis for the other numbers.

1	uno	6	seis
2	dos	7	siete
3	tres	8	ocho
4	cuatro	9	nueve
5	cinco	10	diez

● 11–15

11	once	14	catorce
12	doce	15	quince
13	trece		

● 16-19
Note these one-word forms for 16–19: **diez** becomes **diec**, **y** (and) becomes **i** and they join together with **seis, siete, ocho** and **nueve** to form one word. Note the accent on **dieciséis**.

16	dieciséis	18	dieciocho
17	diecisiete	19	diecinueve

● 20-29
20 veinte
For numbers 21-29 **veinte** drops the **e, y** changes to **i** again, and the unit number is added to form one word. Note the accents on **veintidós, veintitrés** and **veintiséis**.

21	veintiuno	26	veintiséis
22	veintidós	27	veintisiete
23	veintitrés	28	veintiocho
24	veinticuatro	29	veintinueve
25	veinticinco		

- 30-99

We no longer have one-word forms. The tens (30, 40, etc.) are followed by **y** and the unit number. There are no exceptions to this pattern for numbers 30 to 99.

30	treinta	**38**	treinta y ocho
31	treinta y uno	**39**	treinta y nueve
32	treinta y dos	**40**	cuarenta
33	treinta y tres	**50**	cincuenta
34	treinta y cuatro	**60**	sesenta
35	treinta y cinco	**70**	setenta
36	treinta y seis	**80**	ochenta
37	treinta y siete	**90**	noventa

Examples

42 cuarenta y dos; 75 setenta y cinco; 99 noventa y nueve

 **¡Atención!**

- *Note that **y** (and) always goes between the tens and the units column and there are no exceptions.*

- *Note too that **uno** and numbers ending in it (21, 31, etc.) need to agree with the object that follows it or to which it refers:*
  *21 (on its own) **veintiuno***
  *21 (before or referring to a masculine noun) **veintiún**, e.g. **veintiún años de edad***
  *21 (before or referring to a feminine noun) **veintiuna**, e.g. **veintiuna personas***
  *¿Cuántos discos tienes? **Veintiuno**.*
  *¿Cuántas botellas hay? **Veintiuna**.*

B **Hundreds**

- There are two words for 100: **cien** and **ciento**.

Cien is used when the number 100 is used with or to refer to a noun: **cien personas** (100 people); **cien libros** (100 books); **cien pesetas** (100 pesetas).

Ciento is used for the numeral 'one hundred' and to form all other numbers from 101 to 199:

101 ciento uno	150	ciento cincuenta
102 ciento dos	199	ciento noventa y nueve

Note that **y** (and) is not used with hundreds.
You never use **un** with **ciento** or **cien**.

- From 200 upwards, the hundreds have masculine and feminine forms:

200 doscientos/as	600 seiscientos/as
300 trescientos/as	700 setecientos/as
400 cuatrocientos/as	800 ochocientos/as
500 quinientos/as	900 novecientos/as

The pattern is easy to follow. Look at these examples:
434 cuatrocientos treinta y cuatro
817 ochocientos diecisiete

 **¡Atención!**

- *Note **quinientos**, **setecientos** and **novecientos** which are a little different from what you might expect.*
- *Do not confuse **seiscientos** and **setecientos**.*

c **Higher numbers**
  - 1.000 mil
    You never place **un** before **mil**, and **mil** never changes: **mil pesetas** (1.000 pesetas).
    The rest of the pattern is easy to follow:

2.000 dos mil	10.000 diez mil
3.000 tres mil	25.000 veinticinco mil
5.000 cinco mil	

  - In Spanish a full stop (.) is used to separate the thousands and not a comma:
    1.000.000 un millón   2.000.000 dos millones

  - Note that **de** follows **millón** when it is used with a noun: **un millón de libras** (a million pounds).

  - Note also: cientos de... *hundreds of ...*
    miles de... *thousands of ...*

D **Telephone numbers**

There are a number of ways of saying a telephone number:
  - as individual numbers
    727 4174 siete-dos-siete-cuatro-uno-siete-cuatro

- as pairs of numbers
  727 4174 siete-veintisiete-cuarenta y uno-setenta y cuatro

- as groups of numbers
  727 4174 setenta y dos-setenta y cuatro-diecisiete-cuatro
  setecientos-veintisiete-cuarenta y uno-setenta y cuatro

¿Entiendes?

A Match up each number in the box with the correct number in words.

1 ochenta y tres.
2 quinientos uno
3 ciento
4 setecientos catorce
5 sesenta y seis

6 ciento veintitrés
7 trescientos cuarenta y siete
8 mil
9 setenta y nueve
10 novecientos noventa y nueve

| 714 | 123 | 501 | 83 | 999 |
| 79 | 1000 | 100 | 347 | 66 |

B Now write out the following numbers in words.

1 58
2 406
3 685
4 1.722

5 5.295
6 12.700
7 30.890
8 100.000

C Write out these sentences filling in the gaps with the correct number from the box opposite.

1 Hay ..... minutos en ..... hora y un total de ..... segundos.
2 Hay ..... días en ..... semana.
3 Hay ..... meses en ..... año.
4 ..... año tiene ..... estaciones: primavera, verano, otoño e invierno.
5 Hay ..... días en un año.
6 Agosto tiene ..... días.
7 El Rey de España, Juan Carlos, tiene ..... hijos.

una	siete
trescientos sesenta y cinco	un
una	sesenta
tres	un
doce	treinta y un
cuatro	**tres mil seiscientos**

D Compare the telephone numbers with their written form. Say whether they are true or false.

1 719 0627   siete-diecinueve-cero-seis-veintisiete
2 135 8637   uno-tres-cinco-ocho-siete-tres-siete
3 392 8165   tres-noventa y dos-ochenta y uno-setenta y cinco
4 751 6209   siete-cinco-uno-seis-dos-cero-nueve
5 854 1748   ocho-cincuenta y cuatro-dieciséis-cuarenta y ocho

2 Ordinal numbers are the numbers that mean 'first', 'second', 'third', etc. They are adjectives and must therefore agree with the noun:

la primera fila	*the first row*
la segunda guerra mundial	*the second world war*
los primeros asientos	*the first seats*

1st	primero/a	6th	sexto/a
2nd	segundo/a	7th	sé(p)timo/a
3rd	tercero/a	8th	octavo/a
4th	cuarto/a	9th	noveno/a
5th	quinto/a	10th	décimo/a

 **¡Atención!**

- *Note that the ordinal numbers can also be abbreviated in Spanish (especially when you are writing addresses):*
  primero... 1º; cuarta... 4ª

- *Ordinal numbers are mostly used only up to 'tenth'. If any higher ordinal number is required the cardinal number is used after the noun:*
  el siglo **veinte** *(the 20th century)*
  Alfonso **trece** *(Alfonso the 13th)*

- Remember: **Primero** and **tercero** lose the **o** before a masculine singular noun:
  el **primer** piso (the first floor), el **tercer** día (the third day).

- Be careful not to confuse **cuarto** (fourth) and **cuatro** (four).

- Only **primero** is used in dates: el **primero** de abril (the first of April). Otherwise the cardinal numbers are used: el **dos** de mayo, el **diez** de agosto.

Resumen

1 There are two types of numbers:
uno, dos, tres, etc. (cardinal numbers)
primero, segundo, tercero, etc. (ordinal numbers)

2 The cardinal numbers from 31 to 99 in Spanish are written as separate words linked by **y** (and): 37 = **treinta y siete**.

3 **Cien** is used for 100 with or to refer to a noun.
Ciento is used for the numeral 100 and to form all other numbers from 101 to 199.

4 The hundreds from 200 to 900 are adjectives with masculine and feminine forms. Watch out for the irregular forms: **quinientos, setecientos** and **novecientos**.

5 Ordinal numbers are adjectives and agree with the noun they describe.

37 Measures and dimensions

1 There are various ways of saying how wide, long, tall, etc. things are. You can use these expressions to cover certain elements of the GCSE examination (describing your bedroom, describing your family in detail, etc.) and also to give fuller descriptions as required in the higher parts of the GCSE examination.

2 The following expressions are used to describe things. Can you match the Spanish and the English:

1	de largo	a	thick
2	de espeso/grueso	b	tall
3	de ancho	c	long
4	de alto	d	deep
5	de profundo	e	wide

- Now look at how these expressions are used:

Mi dormitorio tiene dos metros de largo y dos metros y medio de ancho.	*My bedroom is two metres long and two and a half metres wide.*
La caja de bombones es grande. Tiene treinta centímetros de largo, veinte de ancho y diez de profundo.	*The sweets box is big. It is 30 centimetres long, 20 wide and ten deep.*

Using the above as a guide, describe your bedroom and an object in it.

- More useful expressions:

lleno (de)	*full (of)*
vacío	*empty*
contiene	*it contains/has*
estar hecho de	*to be made of*

3 Look at this sentence which shows how to describe people. Write down the two verbs used to describe how tall people are and how much they weigh:

Mi hermano mide un metro setenta y pesa ochenta kilos.

You should have written down **mide** and **pesa**. **Mide** comes from the verb **medir**, meaning 'to measure' (stem-changing), and **pesa** comes from the verb **pesar**, meaning 'to weigh'.

¿Entiendes?

A Write out these sentences filling in the gaps with the appropiate part of **medir** or **pesar**. Check your answers.

1 Los niños ..... mucho. Están gorditos.
2 Yo ..... un metro cincuenta. Soy pequeño.
3 ¿Y tú? ¿Cuántos kilos .....?
4 ¿Y de alto, ¿cuánto ..... usted?

4 'Per cent' in Spanish is **por ciento**:
80% = ochenta por ciento
80% of = el/un ochenta por ciento de...

When you have a decimal point in a percentage (and any other number) this is expressed as a **coma** (,) in Spanish:
85.5% = un ochenta y cinco coma cinco por ciento

5 Look at the words and expressions you can use when you want to buy quantities of things:

un kilo (de)	*a kilo (of)*
medio kilo (de)	*half a kilo (of)*
un cuarto de kilo (de)	*a quarter of a kilo (of)*
cuatrocientos gramos (de)	*four hundred grams (of)*
una docena (de)	*a dozen (of)*
un litro (de)	*a litre (of)*
un trozo (de)	*a piece (of)*

6 Look at the questions and answers about changing money and enquiring about prices:

¿A cuánto están los plátanos hoy?/ ¿A cuánto van los plátanos hoy?	*How much are the bananas (at) today?*
A doscientas el kilo.	*200 (pesetas) a kilo.*
¿A cuánto está la libra esterlina hoy?	*What is the rate for the pound sterling today?*
Está a 195 pesetas.	*It's 195 pesetas.*

38 The subjunctive

1   If you go on to study Spanish at a higher level you will definitely need
the subjunctive, as it forms an important part of the Spanish language.
At this stage, you might like to be able to recognise it, and you may
even like to start using one or two examples!
The subjunctive is a different form of the verb that needs to be used at
certain times. It is not a tense. The subjunctive is often referred to as a
'mood', is mostly used under certain conditions and with certain set
phrases, and very often expresses the way you feel.

2   The present subjunctive is formed in the following way:

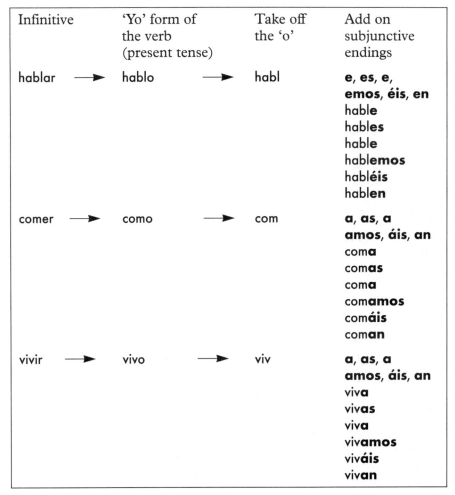

Infinitive	'Yo' form of the verb (present tense)	Take off the 'o'	Add on subjunctive endings
hablar →	hablo →	habl	**e, es, e, emos, éis, en** hable hables hable hablemos habléis hablen
comer →	como →	com	**a, as, a amos, áis, an** coma comas coma comamos comáis coman
vivir →	vivo →	viv	**a, as, a amos, áis, an** viva vivas viva vivamos viváis vivan

An easy way of remembering this is that all the verbs change to behave like their opposites. Therefore, an **-ar** behaves like an **-er** verb, and **-er** and **-ir** verbs behave like **-ar** verbs (again sharing the same endings).

 **¡Atención!**

- *If the verb is stem-changing in the present tense, then it will also be in the subjunctive.*

- *Verbs ending in **-car** change the **c** to **qu** before the subjunctive ending: buscar – busque, busques, busque, busquemos, busquéis, busquen*

- *Verbs ending in **-gar** insert **u** before the subjunctive ending: llegar – llegue, llegues, llegue, lleguemos, lleguéis, lleguen*

3 Some verbs are irregular.

- They are irregular in the first person singular in the present tense and are therefore irregular in the present subjunctive:

conocer ⟶ conozca
decir ⟶ diga
hacer ⟶ haga
oír ⟶ oiga
poner ⟶ ponga
salir ⟶ salga
tener ⟶ tenga
venir ⟶ venga

- There are six verbs that are totally irregular in the present subjunctive:

dar ⟶ dé
estar ⟶ esté
haber ⟶ haya
ir ⟶ vaya
saber ⟶ sepa
ser ⟶ sea

You will find the full forms of these verbs in the Verb Tables.

4 The subjunctive is always used under certain circumstances and with set expressions.

A After verbs of wanting and preferring when the subject of the sentence changes:

Prefiero que tú **hagas** la compra. *I prefer you to do the shopping.*

Queremos que te **quedes**. *We want you to stay.*

B After verbs expressing emotions (joy, sadness, fear, anger, hope, etc.):

Siento que no **puedas** venir. *I'm sorry that you can't come.*

Espero que **tengan** bastante dinero. *I hope they have enough money.*

Temo que **esté** enferma. *I am afraid she is ill.*

C After verbs of commanding or instructing:

Mi madre dice que no **vaya**. *My mother says that I can't go.*

D After a negative or an indefinite sentence (when the sentence is about an unknown person):

No hay nada que **pueda** hacer. *There is nothing I can do.*

No conozco a nadie que **hable** ruso. *I know no one who speaks Russian.*

E After expressions that imply doubt or that something is not probable:

No es cierto que **sepa** donde está. *It's not certain he'll know where it is.*

Dudo que **conozca** a mi padre. *I doubt if he knows my father.*

F After certain conjunctions (see Point 16) which refer to future time such as, **cuando** (when), **en cuanto** (as soon as), **después de que** (after):

Cuando **llegues** al colegio, no digas nada. *When you get to school, don't say anything.*

(NB: You do not use the subjunctive in a question about the future:

¿Cuándo llegarás al colegio? *When will you get to school?*)

G After certain expressions:

es mejor que	*it is best that*
es necesario que	*it's necessary that*
es posible que	*it's possible that*
es imposible que	*it's impossible that*
es probable que	*it's probable that*
sin que	*without*
aunque	*even though*
quizás	*perhaps*
tal vez	*maybe*

¿Entiendes?

A Write out the sentences putting the verb in brackets in the correct form of the present subjunctive.

1 Espero que María (ir) a la discoteca mañana.
2 Quizás Toni (llegar) tarde.
3 Es mejor que tú la (visitar) solo.
4 Mis padres no quieren que mi hermano y yo (salir) esta noche.
5 No creemos que su padre les (dejar) ir a la fiesta.
6 No hay nadie que (poder) ayudarnos.

5 The imperfect subjunctive is used in a similar way to the present subjunctive but when you are talking about events in the past. It is very easy to form provided you know the preterite tense (Point 19) and there are no exceptions.

To form it you remove the **-ron** ending from the **ellos/ellas/Vds.** form of the preterite and add either of two sets of endings:
-ra, -ras, -ra, -ramos, -rais, -ran OR
-se, -ses, -se, -semos, -seis, -sen

hablar ⟶ hablaron ⟶ habla (+ endings)
hablara, hablaras, hablara, habláramos, hablarais, hablaran OR
hablase, hablases, hablase, hablásemos, hablaseis, hablasen
comer ⟶ comieron ⟶ comie (+ endings)
comiera, comieras, comiera, comiéramos, comierais, comieran OR
comiese, comieses, comiese, comiésemos, comieseis, comiesen
querer ⟶ quisieron ⟶ quisie (+ endings)
quisiera, quisieras, quisiera, quisiéramos, quisierais, quisieran OR
quisiese, quisieses, quisiese, quisiésemos, quisieseis, quisiesen

This works for all verbs, regular and irregular.

6 The **-ra** form of the imperfect subjunctive of **querer** (**quisiera** etc.) is commonly used instead of the conditional tense to mean 'would like':
¿Cuántos **quisiera**? *How many would you like?*
Quisiera tres. *I would like three.*

Resumen

1 The subjunctive is a 'mood' rather than a tense, and is very important in Spanish.

2 It is used to express emotions, doubts, wants which involve a change of subject in a sentence, and after certain set expressions that always require the subjunctive (refer back to note 4 for detailed uses).

3 *-ar* verbs 'behave' temporarily like *-er* verbs.
-er and *-ir* verbs 'behave' temporarily like *-ar* verbs.

See note 2 about the formation of the present subjunctive, and note 5 for the imperfect subjunctive.

Answers

Point 1 Using *un, uno* and *una*

¿Entiendes?

A 1 una; una   4 un; una
2 unos   5 uno
3 un   6 unas

Point 2 Using *el, la, los* and *las*

¿Entiendes?

A 1 las escaleras   5 los libros
2 los zapatos   6 las cortinas
3 las tazas   7 los vasos
4 los teléfonos   8 las botellas

B 1 the grandparents *or* the grandfathers
2 the aunts and uncles *or* the aunt and uncle *or* the uncles
3 the brothers and sisters *or* the brothers
4 the cousins

C 1 el lápiz = *the pencil*
2 el ratón = *the mouse*
3 el horno = *the oven*
4 la regla = *the ruler*
5 el banco = *the bank*
6 el reloj = *the watch*
7 la televisión = *the television*
8 la flor = *the flower*

Point 3 Nouns and adjectives

¿Entiendes?

A 1 los perros   6 las voces
2 las capitales   7 las abuelas
3 las narices   8 los mares
4 los relojes   9 los pasteles
5 los jefes   10 las maletas

B
1	una chica alta	6	pelo corto
2	zapatos rojos	7	clases interesantes
3	un perro gordo	8	ojos verdes
4	chicas delgadas	9	un sombrero rosa
5	una calle ancha	10	chicos guapos

C
1	a good man	4	a great man
2	on the first floor	5	Have you got any money?
3	the third boy	6	I haven't got any friends.

Point 4 Adverbs

¿Entiendes?

A
1	fácilmente	5	posiblemente
2	ciertamente	6	atentamente
3	lentamente	7	probablemente
4	estupendamente	8	cuidadosamente

B
1	recientemente	4	probablemente
2	regularmente	5	ciertamente
3	atentamente	6	lentamente

C
1	f	9	b
2	a	10	g
3	j	11	m
4	d	12	o
5	c	13	n
6	h	14	k
7	e	15	l
8	i		

Point 6 The present tense (regular and irregular verbs)

¿Entiendes?

A adoro; llegamos; tomamos; bebo; leo; escucha; llevan; pasamos; estudiamos

Point 7 Reflexive verbs

¿Entiendes?

A
1	os	4	nos
2	se	5	me
3	se	6	te

B   2 A las siete y cuarto me ducho.
   3 A las siete y media me visto.
   4 A las ocho menos cuarto me peino.
   5 Me acuesto a las nueve y media.
   6 Me duermo a las diez.

Point 8 Negatives

¿Entiendes?

A   1 no; ni; ni   5 no
   2 nunca *or* no   6 no
   3 no; nada   7 nunca
   4 no; nadie

Point 9 Stem-changing verbs

¿Entiendes?

A   1 yo empiezo tengo pienso siento me siento me despierto
   tú empiezas tienes piensas sientes te sientas te despiertas
   él/ella/Vd. empieza tiene piensa siente se sienta
   se despierta
   nosotros empezamos tenemos pensamos sentimos
   nos sentamos nos despertamos
   vosotros empezáis tenéis pensáis sentís os sentáis
   os despertáis
   ellos/ellas/Vds. empiezan tienen piensan sienten se sientan
   se despiertan
   2 yo puedo muestro encuentro pruebo me duermo
   me muevo
   tú puedes muestras encuentras pruebas te duermes
   te mueves
   él/ella/Vd. puede muestra encuentra prueba se duerme
   se mueve
   nosotros podemos mostramos encontramos probamos
   nos dormimos nos movemos
   vosotros podéis mostráis encontráis probáis os dormís
   os movéis
   ellos/ellas/Vds. pueden muestran encuentran prueban
   se duermen se mueven

B	me visto	elijo	repito	sirvo	digo
	te vistes	eliges	repites	sirves	dices
	se viste	elige	repite	sirve	dice
	nos vestimos	elegimos	repetimos	servimos	decimos
	os vestís	elegís	repetís	servís	decís
	se visten	eligen	repiten	sirven	dicen

Point 10 Commands

¿Entiendes?

A 1 d   4 b
   2 a   5 c
   3 f   6 e

B 1 pele; corte   5 añada; ponga
   2 pele; corte   6 cocine
   3 fría   7 sirva
   4 bata

Point 11 *Ser* and *estar*

¿Entiendes?

A 1 está
   2 estoy
   3 estás
   4 es

B 1 era; es
   2 estabas
   3 era *or* es
   4 estoy; estaré

Point 12 The future tense

¿Entiendes?

A voy; voy; van; voy; vamos; vamos; van; va; vamos
B Ganarás; será; tendrás; habrá; comprarás; harás; podrás; acabarán; recibirás
C serás; quedará; empezarán; tendrás; enfadarás; tendrás; cogerás; estarás; pasará; trabajarás; necesitarás; cansarás; irás; viajarás

Point 13 A, al, a la, a los, a las

¿Entiendes?

A
1	al	6	a
2	a la	7	a los
3	a la	8	a las
4	a la	9	a los
5	al	10	al

Point 14 De, del, de la, de los, de las

¿Entiendes?

A
1 El dinero es de la familia.
2 Los coches de los trabajadores son de la empresa.
3 La casa de los vecinos es más grande que la casa de Pedro.
4 Yo soy de Madrid, pero mis padres son de la provincia de Gerona.
5 Mi reloj es de oro.

Point 15 Prepositions

¿Entiendes?

A
1	de la	4	de la
2	del	5	de la
3	del		

B
1	enfrente del	4	al lado del
2	al lado del	5	enfrente del
3	enfrente de la		

Point 16 Conjunctions

¿Entiendes?

A
1 Mi hermano es simpático pero es travieso.
2 Estudio ciencias porque me gustan mucho.
3 Mañana vamos al cine o a lo mejor a la discoteca.
4 Voy a comprar un nuevo compact disc y mi amiga también.

B
1	e	4	y
2	o	5	e
3	u		

Point 17 The personal *a*

¿Entiendes?

A The following five sentences require the personal 'a':
1, 3, 4, 7, 10

Point 18 Possessives

¿Entiendes?

A mi; mi; mi; mis; mi; nuestro; mi; su; mi; mis; mi; su; nuestro; tu; vuestro

B
1 mi coche	7 tu hermano
2 nuestra casa	8 sus caramelos
3 tu perro	9 ¿La casa? Es suya.
4 su jardín	10 (Los coches) son vuestros.
5 vuestras hermanas	11 El gato es mío.
6 mis padres	12 (Las llaves) son mías.

Point 19 The preterite tense

Note 3: irregular verbs

1 d   2 g   3 a   4 b and e   5 c   6 b and e   7 h   8 f

Ir and **ser** are the same in the preterite tense.

¿Entiendes?

A
1 visité	4 fui
2 comió	5 fui
3 vieron	6 compró

B hizo; fuimos; pasé; tomé; me bañé; fuimos; conocimos

Point 20 The perfect tense

¿Entiendes?

A
1 Yo he visitado.	5 Vd. ha bajado
2 Tú has comido.	6 Vosotros habéis tenido
3 Nosotros hemos comprado.	7 Ella ha jugado
4 Ellos han bailado.	8 Él ha preguntado

Point 21 The imperfect tense

¿Entiendes?

A
1 d	4 c
2 e	5 b
3 f	6 a

B Examples of descriptions:
- Llevaba gafas y tejanos.
- Corría hacia el coche.
- El coche era blanco y moderno; estaba limpio.
- La chica tenía el pelo largo y rubio.
- Los dos jóvenes salían del banco.
- Llevaban sacos de dinero.
- El chico tenía el pelo corto, rizado y oscuro.
- La chica llevaba camiseta, falda y zapatillas.

Point 22 Making questions

¿Entiendes?

A
1. ¿Cuántos... ?
2. ¿Cómo... ?
3. ¿Cuándo... ?
4. ¿Cuál... ?
5. ¿Por qué... ?
6. ¿Dónde... ?
7. ¿Cuál... ?
8. ¿Quién... ?
9. ¿Cuánto... ?
10. ¿Cómo... ?

B
1	d	7	l
2	a	8	b
3	h	9	i
4	g	10	e
5	k	11	c
6	j	12	f

Point 23 Por and *para*

¿Entiendes?

A
1. por
2. para
3. para
4. para
5. por
6. para
7. por
8. para
9. por
10. para

Point 24 The pluperfect tense

¿Entiendes?

A
1. P – ¿Has ido a España?
2. PL – Ya había visto la película.
3. PL – Había esperado a su padre.
4. PL – Habíamos cogido el barco.
5. P – ¿Ha tenido buenas notas?

6 PL – Había acabado/terminado los deberes.

7 P – He visitado Barcelona.

8 P – Han comido todas las manzanas.

Point 25 The present and imperfect continuous

¿Entiendes?

A 1 Él está bailando.

2 (Ellos) están comiendo.

3 (Mi padre/Él) está durmiendo.

4 (Mi hermano/Él) está jugando (al baloncesto).

5 (El perro) está corriendo por el bosque.

6 (El hombre) está abriendo la puerta (de la tienda).

7 (Mi madre/Ella) está hablando (con su amiga).

8 (Las chicas) están estudiando (para el examen).

B Some possible sentences would be:
Unas chicas estaban charlando.
Un chico y una chica estaban bailando.
Un chico y una chica estaban comiendo.
Los chicos y las chicas estaban divirtiéndose/se estaban divirtiendo.
Dos chicas estaban bebiendo.
Tres chicos estaban escuchando la música.

Point 26 Pronouns and their positions

¿Entiendes?

A Sí, la tengo.
Sí, los tengo.
Sí, los tengo.
Sí, lo tengo.
Sí, las tengo.
Sí, la llevo.
Sí, los tengo.
Sí, los cogí.

B 1 Me lo dijo.   4 Les estaba diciendo.

2 Te los/las compré.   5 Nos los habían dado.

3 Se lo/la di.   6 Os lo/la llevamos.

Point 27 The conditional tense

¿Entiendes?

A iría; tomaría; metería; descansaría; saldría; bebería; comería; haría

Point 28 Expressions with *tener*

¿Entiendes?

B 1 Tenía hambre.
   2 Tiene frío.
   3 (Tú) tienes suerte.
   4 Tenemos dieciocho años.
   5 Vosotros dos teníais sed anoche.
   6 Mañana tendrán prisa.
   7 Tengo ganas de salir.
   8 Mi padre tiene miedo de las arañas.

Point 29 Comparatives and superlatives

¿Entiendes?

A 1 Verdadero   4 Verdadero
   2 Verdadero   5 Verdadero
   3 Falso   6 Falso

B 1 más... que   4 más... de
   2 tan... como   5 tantos... como
   3 menos... que 6 más

Point 30 Expressions using *lo*

Note 2: using 'lo' with an adjective

1 lo importante = the important thing (+)
2 lo peor = the worst thing (−)
3 lo aburrido = the boring thing (−)
4 lo mejor = the best thing (+)
5 lo interesante = the interesting thing (+)
6 lo fácil = the easy thing (+)
7 lo difícil = the difficult thing (−)

Point 31 Expressions using *tener que, hay que, acabar de* and *deber*

¿Entiendes?

A 1 d   4 e
   2 c   5 b
   3 f   6 a

Point 32 Impersonal verbs: expressing likes, dislikes and opinions

Note 1: like and dislike
me gusta(n) mucho ✓ ✓
me gusta(n) ✓
me encanta(n) ✓ ✓ ✓
no me gusta(n) ✗

¿Entiendes?

A 1 g   5 b
     2 e   6 d
     3 a   7 h
     4 f   8 c

B 1 A María, le encantan los museos.
     2 Nos encanta el español.
     3 A ellos, no le gustan nada los deberes.
     4 A mis amigos, les encanta la discoteca.
     5 Me gusta mucho el chocolate.
     6 A mi hermano, no le gusta estudiar.

Point 33 Soler and poder

¿Entiendes?
A 1 f – I usually play football on Saturdays.
     2 d – You can buy cheese in the supermarket.
     3 a – They used to go to Spain on their holidays.
     4 h – She cannot go to the cinema tomorrow.
     5 b – Do you usually watch TV in the evenings?
     6 g – Can one change money in this bank?
     7 c – Can I speak to Ana?
     8 e – He usually goes to bed early on Mondays.

Point 34 Conocer and saber

¿Entiendes?
A 1 conocí   4 sabía
     2 sé   5 conocemos; sabemos
     3 conozco; sé

Point 35 Weather expressions

Note 1: weather pictures

1 Hace viento.
2 Está despejado.
3 Hace calor.
4 Hay tormenta.
5 Hace sol.
6 Está lloviendo.

7 Hace buen tiempo.
8 Hace frío.
9 Está nublado.
10 Hay niebla.
11 Está nevando.
12 Hace mal tiempo.

¿Entiendes?

A   estoy; paso; fui; conocí; es; llama; viene; dice; hace; está; suele; enseñaré; fue; estaba; hacía; pela; tiempo

Point 36 Numbers

¿Entiendes?

A
1 83
2 501
3 100
4 714
5 66

6 123
7 347
8 1000
9 79
10 999

B
1 cincuenta y ocho
2 cuatrocientos seis
3 seiscientos ochenta y cinco
4 mil setecientos veintidós
5 cinco mil doscientos noventa y cinco
6 doce mil setecientos
7 treinta mil ochocientos noventa
8 cien mil

C
1 sesenta; una; tres mil seiscientos
2 siete; una
3 doce; un
4 un; cuatro
5 trescientos sesenta y cinco
6 treinta y un
7 tres

D
1 true
2 false
3 false

4 true
5 false

Point 37 Measures and dimensions

Note 2: describing things

1	c	4	b
2	a	5	d
3	e		

¿Entiendes?

A 1 pesan
   2 mido
   3 pesas
   4 mide

Point 38 The subjunctive

¿Entiendes?

A	1	vaya	4	salgamos
	2	llegue	5	deje
	3	visites	6	pueda

Verb Tables

	Beber	Comer	Conocer	Dar
Present	bebo	como	conozco	doy
	bebes	comes	conoces	das
	bebe	come	conoce	da
	bebemos	comemos	conocemos	damos
	bebéis	coméis	conocéis	dais
	beben	comen	conocen	dan
Preterite	bebí	comí	conocí	di
	bebiste	comiste	conociste	diste
	bebió	comió	conoció	dio
	bebimos	comimos	conocimos	dimos
	bebisteis	comisteis	conocisteis	disteis
	bebieron	comieron	conocieron	dieron
Imperfect	bebía	comía	conocía	daba
	bebías	comías	conocías	dabas
	bebía	comía	conocía	daba
	bebíamos	comíamos	conocíamos	dábamos
	bebíais	comíais	conocíais	dabais
	bebían	comían	conocían	daban
Future	beberé	comeré	conoceré	daré
	beberás	comerás	conocerás	darás
	beberá	comerá	conocerá	dará
	beberemos	comeremos	conoceremos	daremos
	beberéis	comeréis	conoceréis	daréis
	beberán	comerán	conocerán	darán
Present Subjunctive	beba	coma	conozca	dé
	bebas	comas	conozcas	des
	beba	coma	conozca	dé
	bebamos	comamos	conozcamos	demos
	bebáis	comáis	conozcáis	déis
	beban	coman	conozcan	den
Present Participle	bebiendo	comiendo	conociendo	dando
Past Participle	bebido	comido	conocido	dado

	Decir	Empezar (*)	Estar	Haber
Present	digo dices dice decimos decís dicen	empiezo empiezas empieza empezamos empezáis empiezan	estoy estás está estamos estáis están	he has ha hemos habéis han
Preterite	dije dijiste dijo dijimos dijisteis dijeron	empecé empezaste empezó empezamos empezasteis empezaron	estuve estuviste estuvo estuvimos estuvisteis estuvieron	hube hubiste hubo hubimos hubisteis hubieron
Imperfect	decía decías decía decíamos decíais decían	empezaba empezabas empezaba empezábamos empezabais empezaban	estaba estabas estaba estábamos estabais estaban	había habías había habíamos habíais habían
Future	diré dirás dirá diremos diréis dirán	empezaré empezarás empezará empezaremos empezaréis empezarán	estaré estarás estará estaremos estaréis estarán	habré habrás habrá habremos habréis habrán
Present Subjunctive	diga digas diga digamos digáis digan	empiece empieces empiece empecemos empecéis empiecen	esté estés esté estemos estéis estén	haya hayas haya hayamos hayáis hayan
Present Participle	diciendo	empezando	estando	habiendo
Past Participle	dicho	empezado	estado	habido

	Hacer	Hablar	Ir	Jugar (*)
Present	hago	hablo	voy	juego
	haces	hablas	vas	juegas
	hace	habla	va	juega
	hacemos	hablamos	vamos	jugamos
	hacéis	habláis	vais	jugáis
	hacen	hablan	van	juegan
Preterite	hice	hablé	fui	jugué
	hiciste	hablaste	fuiste	jugaste
	hizo	habló	fue	jugó
	hicimos	hablamos	fuimos	jugamos
	hicisteis	hablasteis	fuisteis	jugasteis
	hicieron	hablaron	fueron	jugaron
Imperfect	hacía	hablaba	iba	jugaba
	hacías	hablabas	ibas	jugabas
	hacía	hablaba	iba	jugaba
	hacíamos	hablábamos	íbamos	jugábamos
	hacíais	hablabais	ibais	jugabais
	hacían	hablaban	iban	jugaban
Future	haré	hablaré	iré	jugaré
	harás	hablarás	irás	jugarás
	hará	hablará	irá	jugará
	haremos	hablaremos	iremos	jugaremos
	haréis	hablaréis	iréis	jugaréis
	harán	hablarán	irán	jugarán
Present Subjunctive	haga	hable	vaya	juegue
	hagas	hables	vayas	juegues
	haga	hable	vaya	juegue
	hagamos	hablemos	vayamos	juguemos
	hagáis	habléis	vayáis	juguéis
	hagan	hablen	vayan	jueguen
Present Participle	haciendo	hablando	yendo	jugando
Past Participle	hecho	hablado	ido	jugado

	Leer	Oír	Pedir (*)	Pensar (*)
Present	leo	oigo	pido	pienso
	lees	oyes	pides	piensas
	lee	oye	pide	piensa
	leemos	oímos	pedimos	pensamos
	leéis	oís	pedís	pensáis
	leen	oyen	piden	piensan
Preterite	leí	oí	pedí	pensé
	leíste	oíste	pediste	pensaste
	leyó	oyó	pidió	pensó
	leímos	oímos	pedimos	pensamos
	leísteis	oísteis	pedisteis	pensasteis
	leyeron	oyeron	pidieron	pensaron
Imperfect	leía	oía	pedía	pensaba
	leías	oías	pedías	pensabas
	leía	oía	pedía	pensaba
	leíamos	oíamos	pedíamos	pensábamos
	leíais	oíais	pedíais	pensabais
	leían	oían	pedían	pensaban
Future	leeré	oiré	pediré	pensaré
	leerás	oirás	pedirás	pensarás
	leerá	oirá	pedirá	pensará
	leeremos	oiremos	pediremos	pensaremos
	leeréis	oiréis	pediréis	pensaréis
	leerán	oirán	pedirán	pensarán
Present Subjunctive	lea	oiga	pida	piense
	leas	oigas	pidas	pienses
	lea	oiga	pida	piense
	leamos	oigamos	pidamos	pensemos
	leáis	oigáis	pidáis	penséis
	lean	oigan	pidan	piensen
Present Participle	leyendo	oyendo	pidiendo	pensando
Past Participle	leído	oído	pedido	pensado

	Poder (*)	Poner	Querer (*)	Saber
Present	puedo	pongo	quiero	sé
	puedes	pones	quieres	sabes
	puede	pone	quiere	sabe
	podemos	ponemos	queremos	sabemos
	podéis	ponéis	queréis	sabéis
	pueden	ponen	quieren	saben
Preterite	pude	puse	quise	supe
	pudiste	pusiste	quisiste	supiste
	pudo	puso	quiso	supo
	pudimos	pusimos	quisimos	supimos
	pudisteis	pusisteis	quisisteis	supisteis
	pudieron	pusieron	quisieron	supieron
Imperfect	podía	ponía	quería	sabía
	podías	ponías	querías	sabías
	podía	ponía	quería	sabía
	podíamos	poníamos	queríamos	sabíamos
	podíais	poníais	queríais	sabíais
	podían	ponían	querían	sabían
Future	podré	pondré	querré	sabré
	podrás	pondrás	querrás	sabrás
	podrá	pondrá	querrá	sabrá
	podremos	pondremos	querremos	sabremos
	podréis	pondréis	querréis	sabréis
	podrán	pondrán	querrán	sabrán
Present Subjunctive	pueda	ponga	quiera	sepa
	puedas	pongas	quieras	sepas
	pueda	ponga	quiera	sepa
	podamos	pongamos	queramos	sepamos
	podáis	pongáis	queráis	sepáis
	puedan	pongan	quieran	sepan
Present Participle	pudiendo	poniendo	queriendo	sabiendo
Past Participle	podido	puesto	querido	sabido

	Salir	Ser	Tener (*)	Venir (*)
Present	salgo sales sale salimos salís salen	soy eres es somos sois son	tengo tienes tiene tenemos tenéis tienen	vengo vienes viene venimos venís vienen
Preterite	salí salíste salió salimos salisteis salieron	fui fuiste fue fuimos fuisteis fueron	tuve tuviste tuvo tuvimos tuvisteis tuvieron	vine viniste vino vinimos vinisteis vinieron
Imperfect	salía salías salía salíamos salíais salían	era eras era éramos erais eran	tenía tenías tenía teníamos teníais tenían	venía venías venía veníamos veníais venían
Future	saldré saldrás saldrá saldremos saldréis saldrán	seré serás será seremos seréis serán	tendré tendrás tendrá tendremos tendréis tendrán	vendré vendrás vendrá vendremos vendréis vendrán
Present Subjunctive	salga salgas salga salgamos salgáis salgan	sea seas sea seamos seáis sean	tenga tengas tenga tengamos tengáis tengan	venga vengas venga vengamos vengáis vengan
Present Participle	saliendo	siendo	teniendo	viniendo
Past Participle	salido	sido	tenido	venido

	Ver	Vivir	Volver (*)
Present	veo ves ve vemos veis ven	vivo vives vive vivimos vivís viven	vuelvo vuelves vuelve volvemos volvéis vuelven
Preterite	vi viste vio vimos visteis vieron	viví viviste vivió vivimos vivisteis vivieron	volví volviste volvió volvimos volvisteis volvieron
Imperfect	veía veías veía veíamos veíais veían	vivía vivías vivía vivíamos vivíais vivían	volvía volvías volvía volvíamos volvíais volvían
Future	veré verás verá veremos veréis verán	viviré vivirás vivirá viviremos viviréis vivirán	volveré volverás volverá volveremos volveréis volverán
Present Subjunctive	vea veas vea veamos veáis vean	viva vivas viva vivamos viváis vivan	vuelva vuelvas vuelva volvamos volváis vuelvan
Present Participle	viendo	viviendo	volviendo
Past Participle	visto	vivido	vuelto